HAREWOOD MASTERPIECES

English Watercolours and Drawings

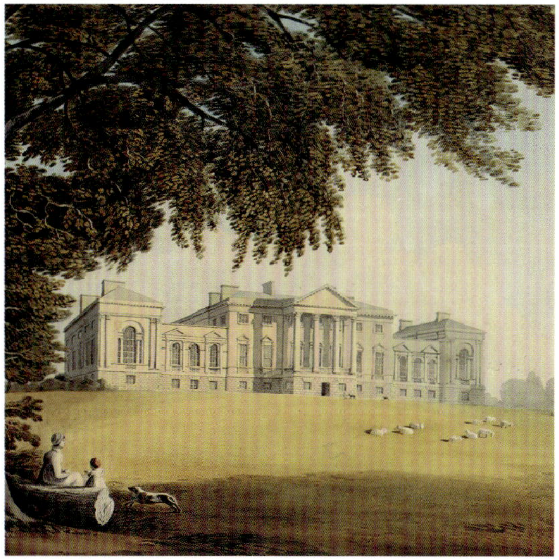

David Hill

HAREWOOD

Published in 1995 by
Harewood House Trust Ltd.
The Estate Office, Harewood Leeds LS17 9LQ
Registered Charity No. 517753

British Library Cataloguing in Publication Data.
A CIP catalogue record for this book is available from the British Library.

ISBN 0-9521021-7-X cloth
ISBN 0-9521021-8-8 paperback

Title page: *John Varley – **Harewood House from the South West,** 1803 (detail).*

Typeset in 11/14pt Garamond
Designed and produced by Designers and Partners Ltd., Oxford.

Printed by and with the generous support of Watmoughs Financial Print Ltd., Bradford and London.

CHRISTIE'S

Contents

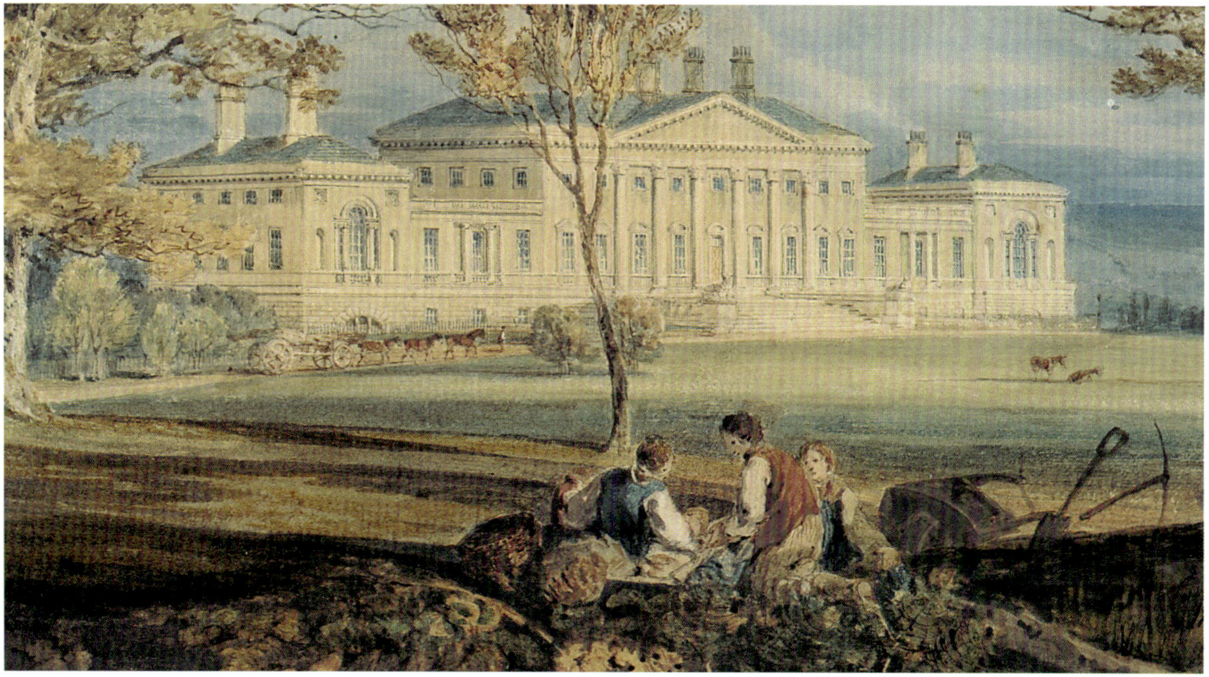

J.M.W. Turner –
Harewood House from the North East, *1797 (detail).*

Foreword

THIS IS THE FIRST of what we hope may become a series of authoritative guides to the collections at Harewood and it gives me great pleasure to introduce it.

Until relatively recently, the better known watercolours were on public display in what was then my mother's sitting room whilst others were hung in private apartments. However, major refurbishment and re-hanging has meant that there are now two rooms devoted to their display on a rotating basis. Light levels and environmental conditions can be fully controlled and the watercolours protected for future generations.

This book and the associated exhibition highlights the early relationship between Harewood and the great English watercolourists of the late eighteenth and early nineteenth centuries. My collateral ancestor, Edward, Viscount Lascelles, was a considerable patron of the arts, commissioning to J.M.W. Turner, Thomas Girtin, John Varley and John Sell Cotman to paint various aspects of the house. Edward was one of Turner's earliest patrons; the artist was only 22 years old went he came to Harewood in 1797, a visit which produced a number of highly accomplished works described in detail by Dr David Hill.

In mid nineteenth century my great grandfather saw fit to dispose of many of Edward's

The North Front of Harewood House.

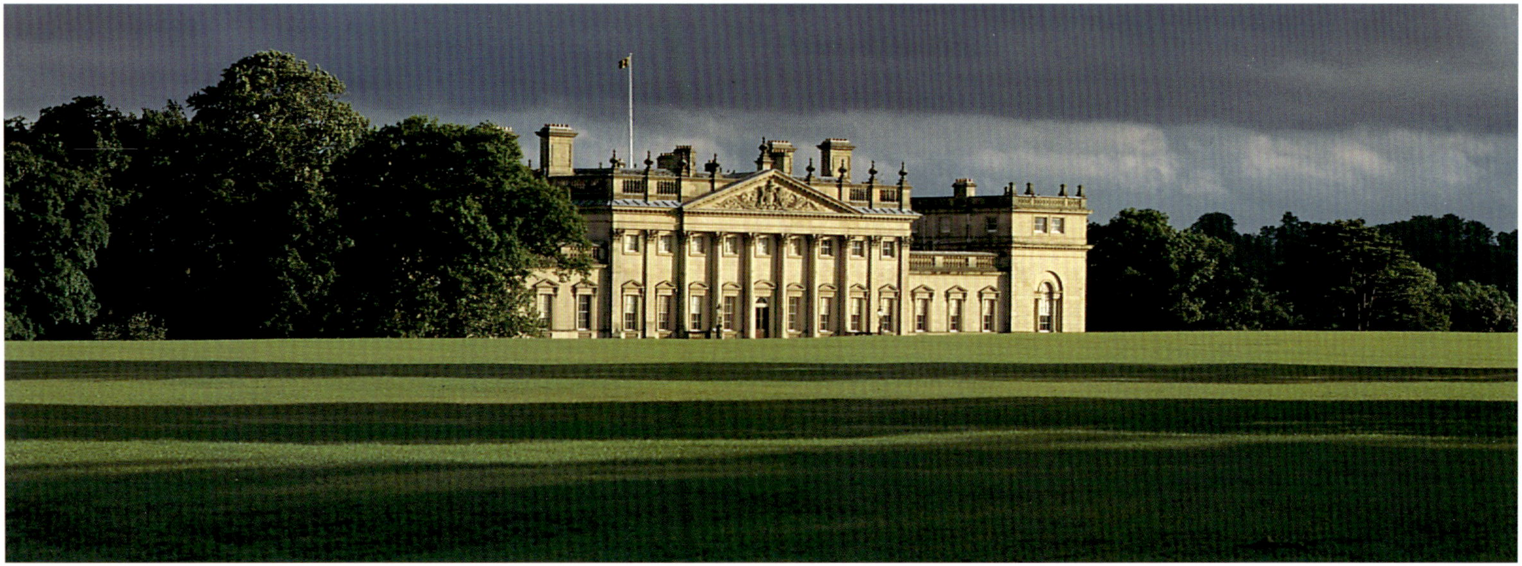

watercolours, apparently because he was afraid they might fade. It has been the task of later generations of the family to bring as many of these works as possible back to the house and to acquire other examples of Harewood's association with the watercolour tradition. My parents, the 6th Earl of Harewood and Princess Mary, were particularly successful. They were given Turner's *Harewood House from the South East* as a wedding present by the Countess of Wharncliffe in 1922. There is evidence that they presented each other with watercolours at family birthdays and Christmases. In recent years I myself have been fortunate in re-acquiring both John Varley's *Harewood House from the South East and Harewood Castle,* as well as purchasing such interesting works as Francis Stevens' *View of Harewood House from a distance.*

At Harewood, now cared for by a charitable Trust, we have taken this opportunity to re-create the impression of an early nineteenth century connoisseur's cabinet, rather in the manner that Edward and his contemporaries might have displayed the work. For inspiration we used a watercolour by Turner of the collection of a contemporary collector of watercolours, Walter Fawkes. We re-decorated the rooms following in broad terms the colour schemes suggested in that work and where practicable restored the original gilt neo-classical frames. Several of the works, including the Turners, had been re-framed in modern times and these have been re-framed and close mounted in the style of the period.

The Harewood House Trust is especially grateful to Christie's for their generous help in printing this publication and in helping to realise a long-held ambition of ours to display the watercolours to full advantage in conditions best suited to their presentation, interpretation and long-term conservation.

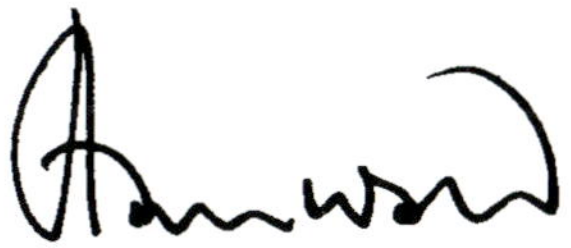

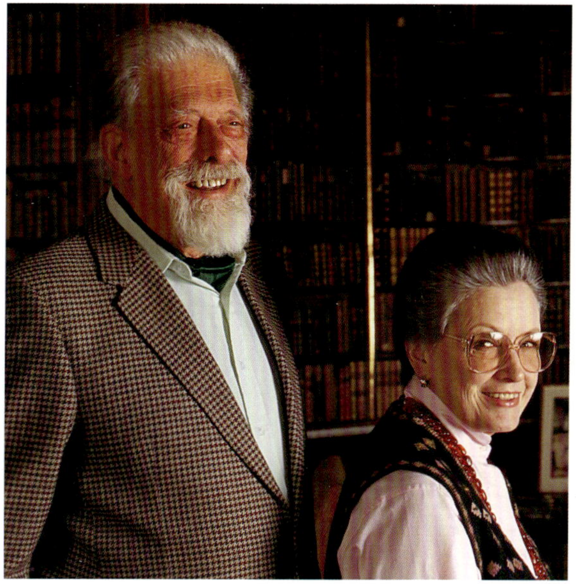

The Earl and Countess of Harewood photographed in the Library at Harewood House.

Introduction

ENGLISH WATERCOLOUR is one of the greatest achievements in the history of art. At the end of the eighteenth century and beginning of the nineteenth century a generation of artists including Joseph Mallord William Turner, Thomas Girtin, John Sell Cotman and John Varley developed the medium as a major vehicle of artistic expression and extended the possibilities of its use to a degree unparalleled before or since. It is perhaps less widely known that Harewood House played an important role in that development. Between 1795 and 1814 Edward Lascelles, the son of the first Earl of Harewood, was one of the most important collectors of work by young artists. In the case of at least two of these, Turner and Girtin, it can be claimed that their association with the house and the Lascelles family was vital to the development of their art, and was thus instrumental in bringing about the revolution in the watercolour medium for which they are famed.

Harewood House was built by Edwin Lascelles and completed in 1771.[1] By 1795 it was 'deservedly ranked with the first buildings in the kingdom'.[2] Its fame rested principally on its architecture and interiors but in terms of works of art it seems to have been somewhat late in its development. On 29 August 1801 the artist Joseph Farington recorded in his diary that he 'Saw Lord Harewood's House – It is built of stone, and is beautifully situated on the side of sloping ground at the bottom of which a fine river passes. The view of the country is very extensive, and exhibits all the riches of cultivation. The House is a very good one, and the rooms comfortable and seem made for use'.[3] It was not, he discovered, too lengthy a task to make a complete inventory of the paintings he found within, noting four Italianate compositions, three local scenes and eight portraits.[4] By comparison with most country houses of this time, Harewood must have seemed to possess a disappointingly poor collection. If Farington was too tactful to say so, then the Revd. Richard Warner who visited Harewood the following year, was not: 'Nothing within interests the mind; no production of the arts, unless the labours of the gilder and upholsterer may be considered as deserving that character'.[5]

Edwin did not entirely neglect the visual arts. The decorations of the house include paintings by Angelica Kaufmann and local subjects by Nicholas Dall. A watercolour by him of *Harewood House from the South East* (*Ill. 1*) dated 1783 forms part of the collection at Harewood.[6] In style it shows an interest in contemporary artists such as Paul Sandby in the use of bodycolour to give the distances solidity, and in the detail of the foreground cattle and feathery foliage indicates a knowledge of the work of Gainsborough. In its sweeping lines running up to the house, and the swirl of cloud above, it even anticipates the work of Girtin, Turner and Varley. The drama perhaps exceeds the bounds of propriety in the treatment of Almscliffe Crag in the centre distance which rears out of Wharfedale like a volcano, but the watercolour is nevertheless a sophisticated accomplishment, suggesting an active familiarity with contemporary landscape, and since the same view was painted by many of the artists who worked at Harewood it serves as a yardstick by which the evolution of watercolour can be measured.

A number of artists came to visit Edwin's newly completed house. Michael Angelo Rooker must have been one of the first, for in 1773 he

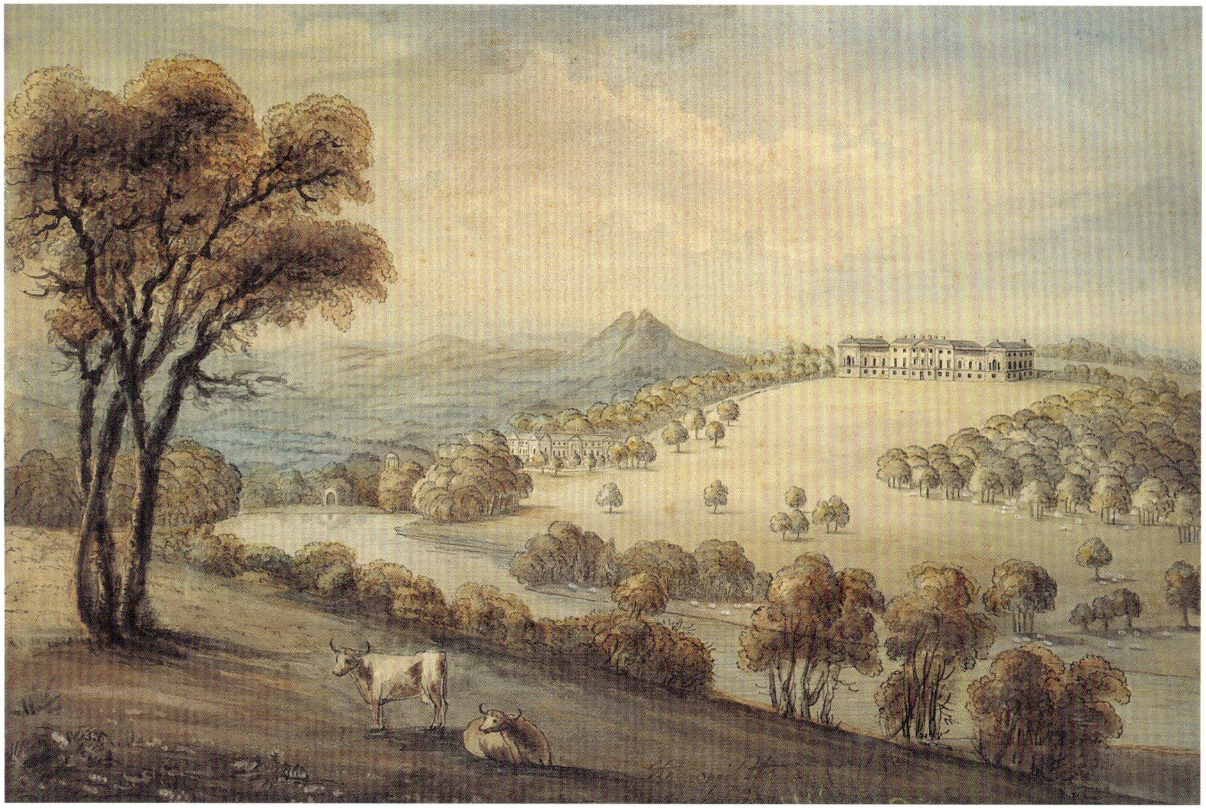

1. Edwin Lascelles – ***Harewood House from the South East,*** *1783. Painted not long after the completion of the house. The same view was painted by many of the artists who worked at Harewood.*

exhibited at the Royal Academy a now-untraced painting of 'Harewood House in the county of York, the seat of Edwin Lascelles, Esq.'[7] In 1774 Thomas Sandby RA, elder brother of the more famous Paul Sandby, made a tour to Yorkshire and made watercolours of the north and south fronts of Harewood, as well as an informed critique of the architecture.[8] In 1778 the leading architectural and antiquarian draughtsman of the day, Thomas Malton, visited the house and made a pair of watercolours.[9] These survive at Harewood in remarkably fresh condition (*Ills. 2,3*) and demonstrate very well the most refined manner of tinted drawing of the age. The pictures are precisely drawn, clear-cut and decisive in line, and chisel out the form and detail of the house with firmness of

2. Thomas Malton – ***Harewood House from the North East,*** *1778. Malton was Turner's master, and his refined elegant style was typical of his age. Malton's architectural detail is more accurate than Turner's later treatment of the same view.*

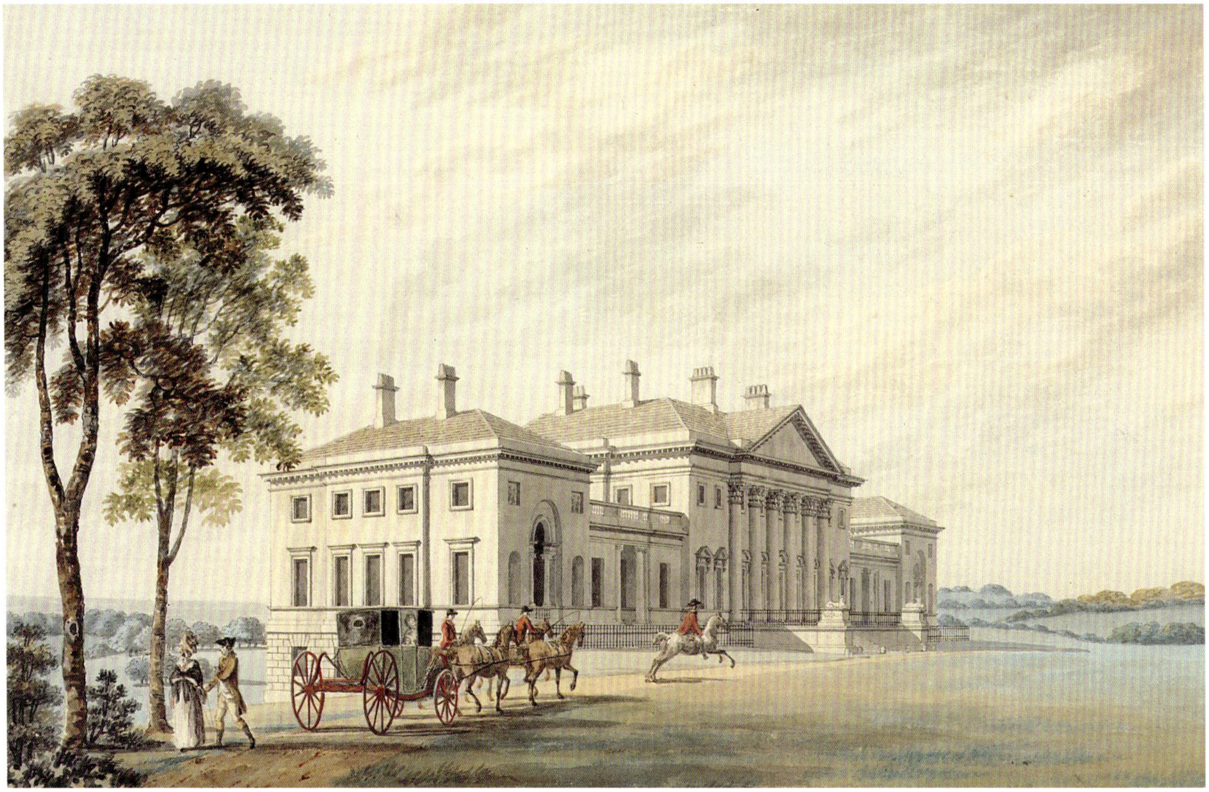

knowledge. The colouring is fresh and the detail of the figures shows the family and friends enjoying the benefits of their newly-finished domain. A jaunty coach arrives at the north front, while the party on the lawns before the south front seems to include Lady Worsley, the celebrated stepdaughter of Edwin Lascelles, dressed in the same red outfit and hat that she wears in Sir Joshua Reynolds's portrait of her elsewhere in the house.[10] Malton became extremely successful with this kind of work, and developed a thriving London studio supplying work for both private clients and publication. His manner formed the example against which the Romantic watercolourists forged their own styles, and the greatest of these, Turner, began his career in Malton's studio.[11]

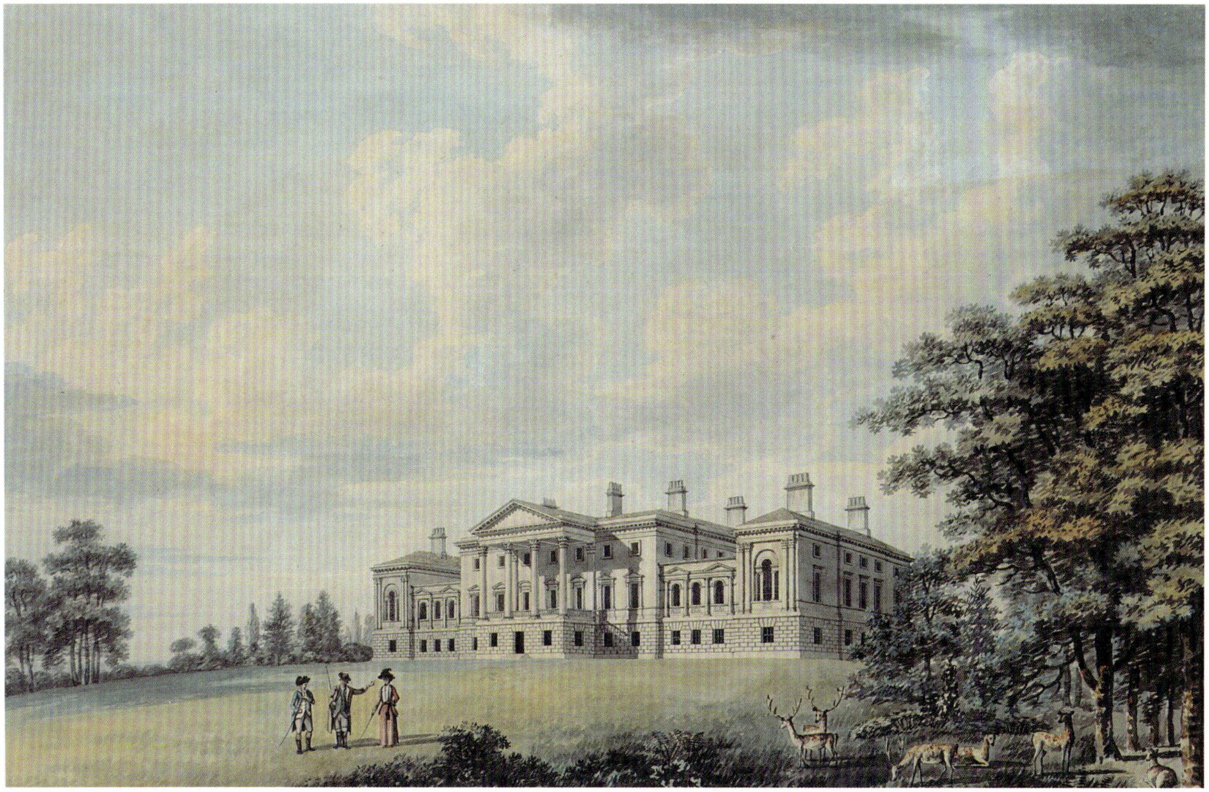

3. Thomas Malton – ***Harewood House from the South East,*** *1778. Malton shows the family enjoying their new domain. The lady in the red suit is perhaps Lady Worsley, the celebrated stepdaughter of Edwin Lascelles.*

Edward Lascelles - Patron of Watercolours

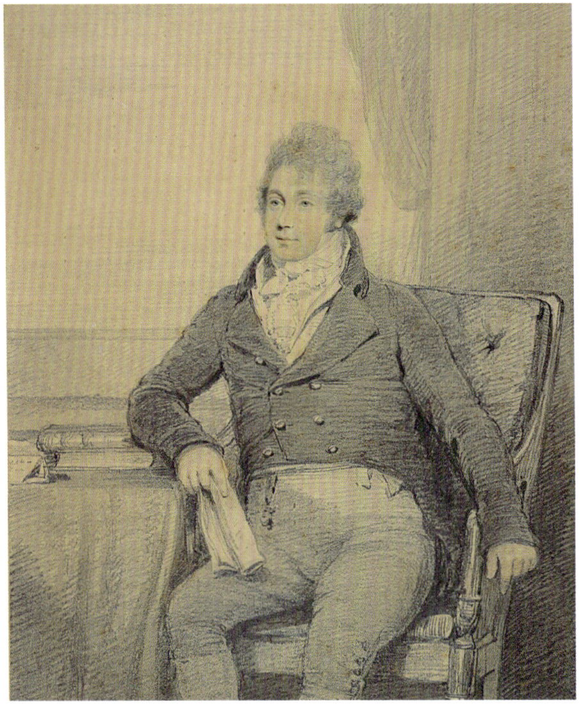

4. Henry Edridge – ***Edward Lascelles, the younger,*** *1805. The son of the 1st Earl of Harewood, and one of the leading beaux of the Regency Age, Edward was one of the most important collectors of the work of young British artists.*

THE PRINCIPAL ARCHITECT of the Harewood collection of watercolours was Edward Lascelles, the son of the 1st Earl of Harewood. The father, Edward Lascelles the elder, inherited Harewood on Edwin's death in 1795. In 1796 he was created Lord Harewood and in 1812 Earl and the title has descended through seven generations to the present day. Edward Lascelles the younger died six years before his father in 1814, but during his life of fifty years he was one of the most wealthy and fashionable of Regency beaux, and one of the most important collectors of work by young English avant-garde artists. It so happens that the principal avant-garde medium at this time was watercolour, and the two most outstanding young talents Turner and Girtin. The father, on the other hand, seems, as perhaps one might expect, to have devoted himself more to the managing of the Harewood fortune than the spending of it and his purchases seem to have been mostly for the enrichment of the house. Fortunately we may come to know the two extremely well. Their day-to-day purchases are recorded in fascinating detail in six leather-bound personal account books now housed at the City Archives department in Leeds.[12] These books document Lascelles patronage of Turner, Girtin, and many other artists including A.W.Callcott, John Varley, William Daniell, Paul Sandby and Henry Edridge. The payments to artists occur in a lively setting of accounts with morris dancers, musicians, hairdressers, tailors and perfumers: subscriptions to the opera, a library, Bowyer's 'History of England', the 'Historic Gallery', 'Ancient Music', 'Oriential Views', novels, Almanacs, botanies and the Bible; club dues, Sunday concerts, dinners and Schweppes soda water. Both father and son shared a fondness for fine china, and a talent for losing money at cards, and payments for wine, truffles, confectionery and warm baths at Harley Street show that both enjoyed all the comforts of their age. One of these comforts was that of being able to sleep unmolested, there being a payment 'To Benj. Teffin for destroying Bugs in June 1789'.[13]

The taste of Edward the elder seems to have inclined most to music, beginning a tradition conspicuously inherited by his present descendant. The account books record frequent payments to musicians for performances and teaching his children. His interest in painting, however, is documented by his close association with the portrait painter John Hoppner.[14] He further encouraged an interest in the visual arts in his children, there being a number of payments for lessons in painting and drawing. Samuel Alken was paid £11.2.6 for his services as drawing master in 1790,[15] John Glover £7.7.0 for twelve lessons in 1795,[16] and George Barret £6.5.9 for his services in the same office in 1797.[17] Edward the elder's principal contribution to the visual arts at Harewood, however, was to commission from Turner the two oils of *Plompton Rocks* which hang still in their original situation in the library. These were commissioned to fill the space left by two doors which it had been decided to remove, and Turner made his studies for the two paintings on a visit to Harewood in 1797. The payment for the pair is recorded on 14 June 1798: 'Wm Turner for 2 Views of Plompton & Case for Do...£32.9.0',[18] which works out at 15 guineas each for the paintings plus 19 shillings for the case. The visit as we shall see was to prove seminal for Turner, but it was Edward Lascelles the younger who first met Turner and encouraged him in his association with Harewood.

Edward Lascelles the younger cultivated a flamboyant style. In an era noteworthy for its extravagance he even rivalled the Prince of Wales, not entirely to the latter's satisfaction. On 25 January 1796 Farington recorded: 'Young Mr Lascelles of Harewood House is reckoned very like the Prince of Wales. – The Prince is not pleased at it. He calls Lascelles the Pretender. Making a remark on a portrait painting of him by Hoppner He desired an alteration, at present said He "It is more like the Pretender." At Brighton the Prince has been struck on the shoulder familiarly with a "Ha Lascelles how is it?" To which He has returned a marked look of disapprobation'.[19] The portrait by Hoppner hangs at Harewood today and from this, and from the portrait drawing by Henry Edridge (*Ill. 4*), we can derive a good idea of the Pretender's style. Farington further recorded that in 1795 Edward made a sketching trip with Hoppner: 'He went with young Mr Lascelles, who has a taste for the arts, & has practiced a little, several excursions to see remarkable places. Bolton bridge is a very picturesque spot'.[20] Some interesting evidence of Edward's having practiced a little

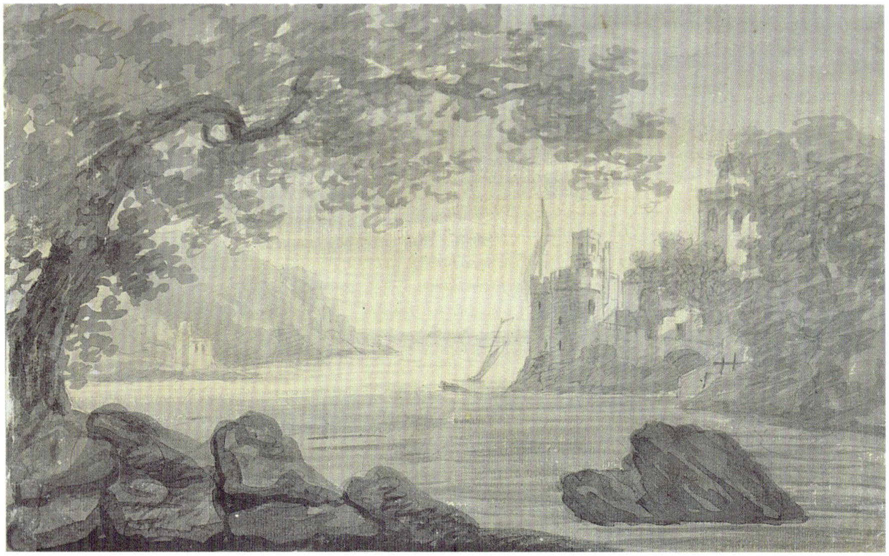

5. Edward Lascelles – ***Dartmouth Castle, Devonshire,*** *c.1800. Edward Lascelles took lessons from Thomas Girtin. From an album of his work in the library at Harewood.*

survives to us in the form of an album of watercolours by him in the library at Harewood (*Ill.5*) The subjects are mostly views in Devon, and painted in a style reminiscent of the monochromatic manner adopted by Girtin and Turner while young men. From these and from his account books we can build up a detailed record of his tastes and activities as one of the most interesting patrons of modern British art of his day.

His interest in collecting pictures lasted roughly twelve years from 1796 to 1808, and during this time he managed to build up an outstanding collection of contemporary British artists. A catalogue of the pictures at his London House in Hanover Square, taken sometime after his death in 1814, testifies to this and offers rare documentation for a complete collection in this period. The list which is here published as an Appendix (p.57), includes eleven works by Turner, nineteen by Thomas Girtin, and others by Paul Sandby, John Varley, John Sell Cotman, William Havell, Peter de Wint, John Smith, Hoppner, A.W.Callcott, Zuccarelli, De Court, Cotes, Holbein, Payne, Pillemans and Vernet. Most of these were sold by the 4th Earl at Christie's on 1 May 1858, and the watercolours that can be seen today at Harewood are those which subsequent generations of the family have re-acquired over the years. Much work remains to be done on identifying the whereabouts of many items from the collection, and it is hoped future research will provide the material for subsequent exhibitions at the house.

Among the various interests represented in the account books of Edward the younger is a taste for picturesque touring and in the autumn of 1795 he paid £32.10.0 for 'Expences on a tour to the Lakes, Servants, Horses &c', £10.0.0 for 'Expences to Ripon, Studley &c' and five guineas for 'Expences to Studley and Hackfall'.[21] He was at Cassiobury Park, the seat of the Earl of Essex, over Christmas 1795 and early in 1796 he began his collection of pictures. On 1 January he paid £7.17.6 to a 'Mr. Daniel', probably William

Daniell the topographical artist, for Prints[22] and on 1 March to Paul Sandby, one of the most distinguished watercolourists of this moment, £31.10.0 for two large drawings;[23] on 18 May he paid W Payne £8.8.0 for drawings,[24] and on 18 June the manufacturer Newman £8.10.6 for Colours,[25] showing that not only was he exercising his purse in his taste for the arts but that he was still 'practising a little'.

The account books also testify to the friendship between the Lascelles family and the Capel family, Earls of Essex, of Cassiobury Park near Watford in Hertfordshire. Both Edwards, father and son, made regular visits to Cassiobury, and in 1799 Edward the younger visited the Capels' country seat at Hampton Court, Herefordshire.[26] The son of the 4th Earl of Essex, the Viscount Malden, was at the centre of a circle of patronage concentrated on a group of young artists who were working at an informal 'Academy' run by Dr Thomas Monro at his home in Adelphi Terrace in London.[27] The Harewood collection contains two examples of Turner's work for Dr Monro, typically monochromatic versions of Italian subjects. Through such repetitive work Turner and Girtin acquired a thorough grounding in the vocabulary and grammar of artistic language. Monro had a large collection of watercolours by eighteenth century English artists, and invited young aspirants to his home in the evenings to study and copy works from his collection. Among these were Girtin and Turner, who it is recorded sometimes sat together while one pencilled in the outlines and the other applied the colour. Viscount Malden seems to have got to know both at this time, and in fact is recorded as having rescued Girtin from jail whence he had been sent as a recalcitrant apprentice, having come to a serious disagreement with his master the watercolourist Edward Dayes.[28] It is likely that it is through Viscount Malden, and his visits to Cassiobury, that Edward the younger came to be introduced to the work of the two young tyros, for shortly after this time the account books record that he bought his first work from Turner, paying three guineas for a work on 17 May 1797.[29] Whatever else might be the case, we certainly have to discount the oft-repeated tradition that Lascelles simply chanced upon Turner sketching in the park at Harewood one day, for Turner had absolutely no need to seek patrons in such an uncertain, haphazard and romantic manner.

Turner and Harewood

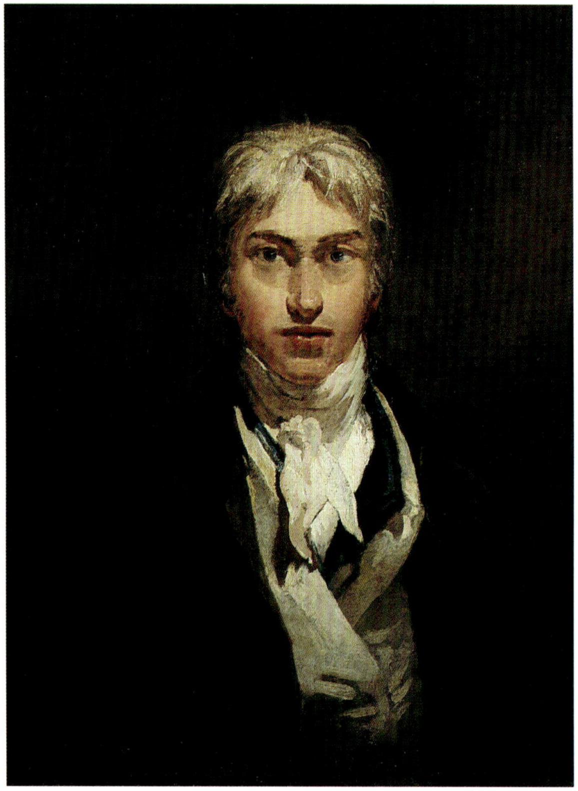

*6. J.M.W. Turner – **Self portrait,** 1796. The artist aged twenty-one, at the threshold of his success. (Courtesy of the Trustees of the Tate Gallery, London)*

By the time Edward Lascelles bought his first work from Turner, the artist, although just twenty-two years of age, was already quite well established (*Ill. 6*). He was born in Maiden Lane, Covent Garden, the son of a hairdresser, entered the Royal Academy schools in 1789, and exhibited works at the Royal Academy from 1790. The Harewood collection includes an example of his early work, a small watercolour of *Windsor Castle from the Forest* (*Ill.7*), made probably around 1794.[30] Although this is a late acquisition, it exhibits a number of features which were to come to the fore in his work for Lascelles. It is particularly noteworthy for being as much concerned with the foreground trees and shepherd as with Windsor Castle, which is thrust into the far distance.[31] Most of his early exhibits, however, were architectural and antiquarian in character, views of abbeys and castles, for which he had earned favourable notices from the reviewers, introducing a dramatic language of atmosphere, chiaroscuro and scale more associated with Rembrandt and Piranesi than traditional British draughtsmanship. Indeed it was an example of just this kind of work which marks Lascelles' first purchase, an *Interior of Westminster Abbey*,[32] now in the British Museum, which he had exhibited at the Royal Academy in 1796. It was for his work as an architectural draughtsman that in 1795 Lascelles's friend, Viscount Malden had commissioned a series of views of his Herefordshire country seat, Hampton Court,[33] and it seems very likely that it was on the strength of these that Edward Lascelles commissioned for himself a similar series of watercolours of Harewood House.

Turner came north to Yorkshire in the summer of 1797 to make his studies for the watercolours. The trip provided him with a springboard from which to launch a tour which took him through Yorkshire, Durham, Northumberland and the Lake District before recrossing the Pennines to Harewood. On the road he filled two large leather-bound sketchbooks[34] with over one hundred and sixty drawings and watercolours of abbeys, priories, castles, churches, towns, mountains and lakes. Yet even though Harewood lay at the end of an itinerary of three hundred miles, Turner's enthusiasm for sketching was still as fresh when he arrived there as when he started out. Twenty drawings in the Turner Bequest at the Tate Gallery[35] testify to the energy and seriousness with which he treated his subject, taking views of the house both in close-up and from the park; Harewood Castle from both inside and out, and also finding time to visit the picturesque nearby sites of Plompton Rocks and Spofforth Castle. He made his sketches of the house and Plompton not in the sketchbooks but on separate sheets of paper, and unfortunately these have been subject to considerable abuse, both in Turner's own studio, where they became paint-spattered and dirty, and in the Turner Bequest where they were stuck down roughly on pieces of card. The full significance of this unpromising-looking bundle of scruffy glue-impregnated sheets only became apparent when they were identified as showing Harewood in 1980,[36] and they can now be seen as the basis of some of his most important early work.

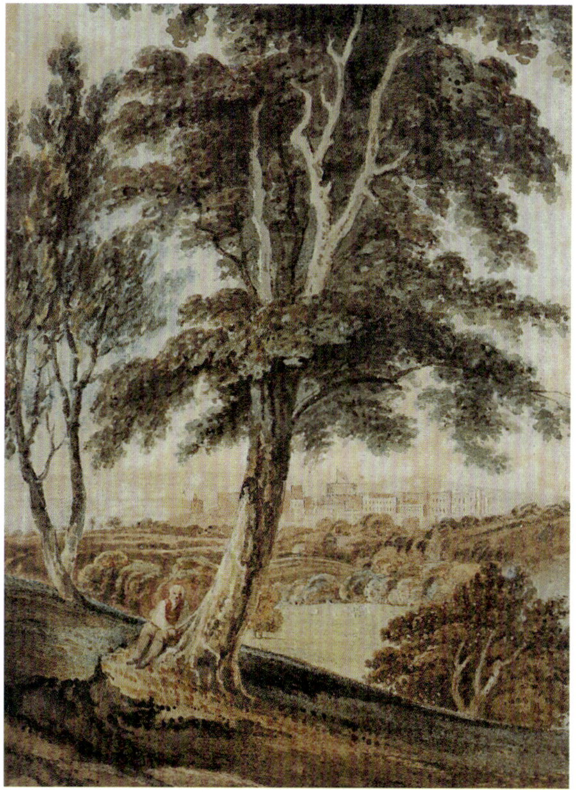

7. J.M.W. Turner – ***Windsor Castle from the Forest,*** *c.1794. An early watercolour, in which Turner's interest in the landscape setting of his subject is already becoming evident.*

Turner was more interested in the landscape setting of Harewood House than in the details of its architecture, and the Turner Bequest sketches show that he stopped to make only one close-up study of the house[37] before he set out into the park to make more expansive views The planting by Capability Brown in the 1760s would have been well established by 1797, and worthy of artistic

*8. J.M.W. Turner – **Harewood House from the North East,** 1797. Edward Lascelles paid 10 guineas for this picture in November 1797. Turner was always interested in he working lives of the people in his landscapes.*

contemplation, and Turner responded with his most detailed pencil work, setting down every minutia of field, park and hill. One of the reasons that these sketches were not identified earlier is that in most of them Turner sketched in only the faintest outline of the house, preferring instead to concentrate on the surroundings. Before Turner set out for Harewood in 1797, *The Times* in reviewing his exhibits at the Academy that year, described his 'direct walk of...profession'[38] as that of architectural draughtsman, but the skeletal indications of the house in these drawings suggest that his feelings for landscape were now beginning to take precedence in his imagination.

The immediate results of Turner's visit to Harewood were recorded in the account books on 21 November 1797 when Edward Lascelles the younger 'paid Mr Turner for two drawings...£21.0.0'.[39] These can be identified as *Harewood House from the North East* and *Harewood House from the South West*, both at the house today (*Ills. 8, 9*). The pair looks back to the work that Turner had earlier made for Viscount Malden of Hampton Court, Herefordshire. The similarities of concept, angle of view and viewing distance suggest that Turner used his experience at Hampton Court as the basis of his work at Harewood. If Edward Lascelles was expecting a simple repeat of the formula that Turner had already used, however, then he was in for an agreeable surprise. The colour saturation of the new work, the density of its paintwork, and assured effects of light and weather show that Turner had made rapid progress in terms of both technique and ambition in the two years or so that separated the two commissions. There were also signs of the direction in which Turner's art was now progressing. A nascent interest in landscape *per se* is evident in the way that he opened up the composition of *Harewood House from the North East* at the right to carry the eye past the house and into the landscape beyond, thus giving a sense of the three-dimensional geography in which the house was situated. In *Harewood House from the South West* he adopted a more distant viewpoint of the house, looking out at evening over the lake with a small boat sailing, sheep grazing on the grassy slopes leading up to the house, and in the foreground, cattle ruminating quietly in the shade beneath the trees. Turner was also developing the human interest of his pictures, and introduced a reed-cutter into the latter picture, together with a child sleeping on the warm ground, no doubt about to make their way home at the end of the day.

Turner's development in relation to the more conventional forms of country house portraiture is particularly evident in the comparison of *Harewood House from the North East* with the earlier watercolour of the same view by Thomas Malton. As late as 3 May 1797, shortly before he set off for the north of England, *The Times* could

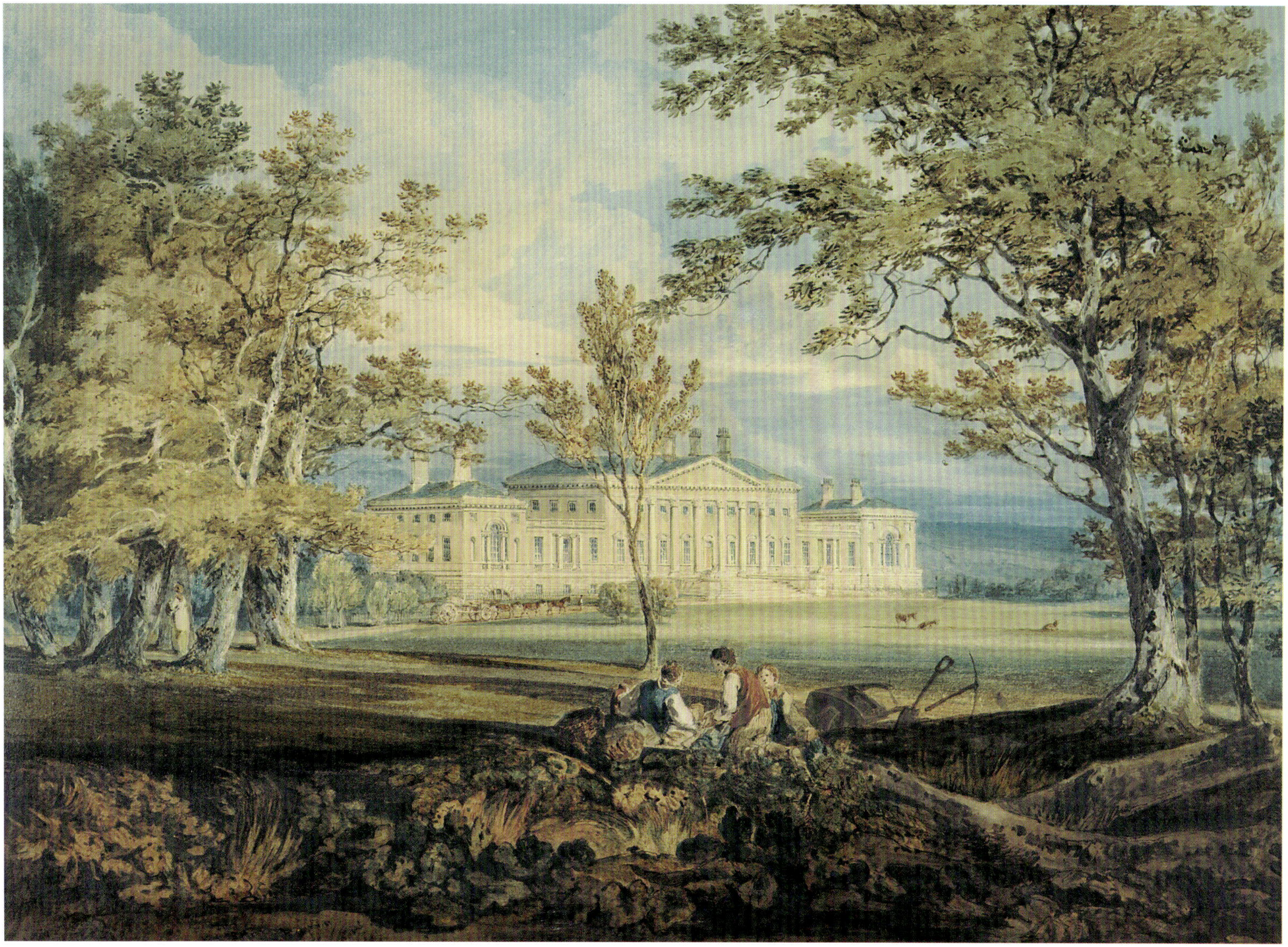

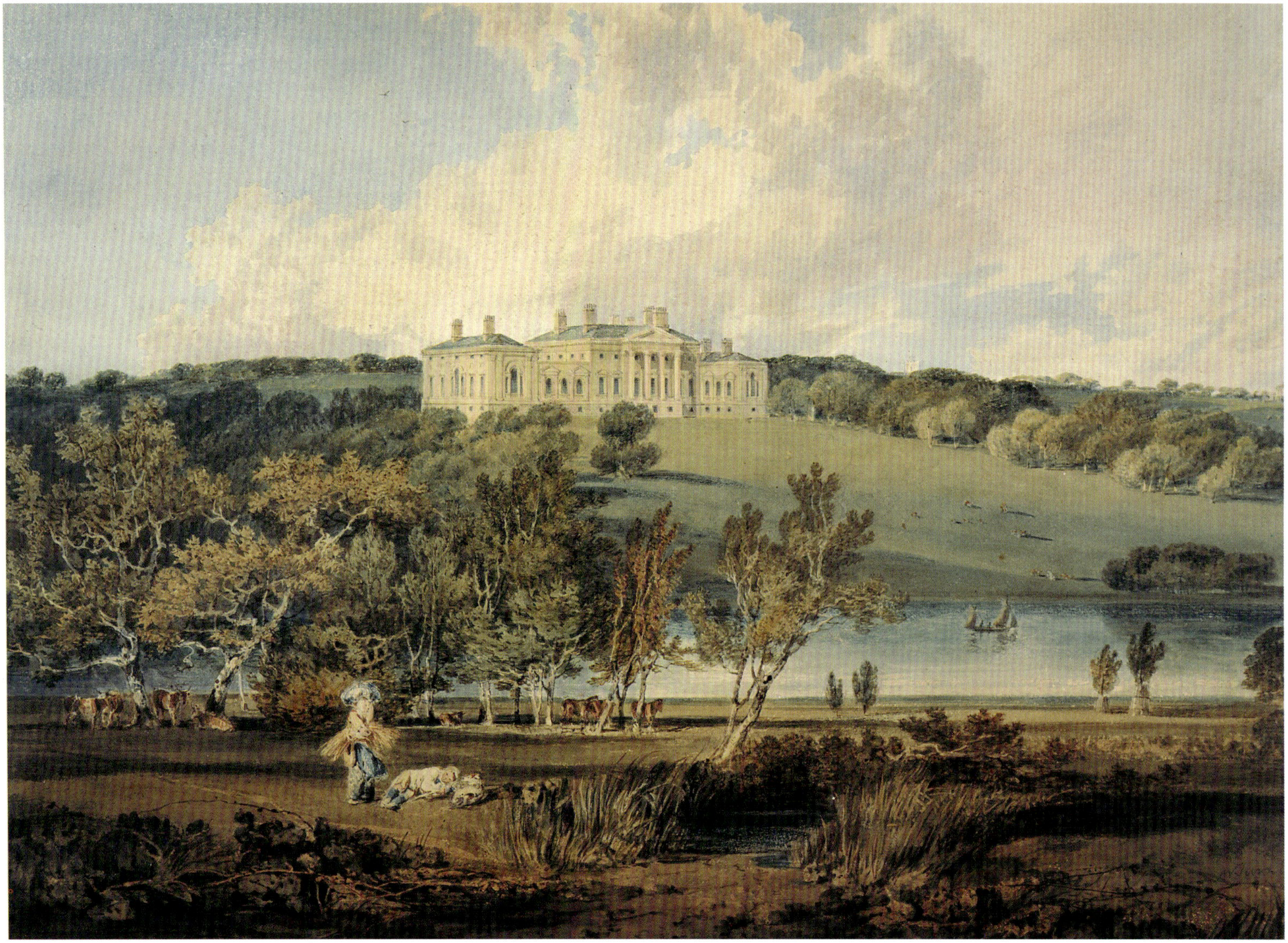

still describe him as a 'Pupil of Mr Malton'.[40] It is possible that Turner chose the same view as his ex-master in this case to demonstrate the maturity of his own development. The comparison is worth considering closely.

Clearly the Turner is the larger, altogether more substantial production, technically more adventurous in its use of the medium and in the solidity of its colour. The Malton belongs to a different age, and its author, who had made his career as an architectural draughtsman, had developed a highly trained and accurate eye for architectural detail. It is therefore not surprising that Malton's drawing can be relied on for matters of fact more than Turner's, and comparison reveals that Turner omitted the shallow bay which relieves and enlivens the east wall of the pavilion and main house. In fact it can be contended that in matters of architectural drawing and in terms of the impression of authority of knowledge, the Malton makes the Turner seem a little uncertain. To eighteenth century eyes the control suggested by Malton's refined tints would have seemed a positive virtue, cultured and cerebral, as one critic has put it, 'communicating a specific class of intelligence to a specific person or class'.[41] The paintwork of Turner might well have seemed somewhat over-bold, and even coarse. And there were many critics to say so. Even into the early years of the nineteenth century many shared the view that his work was ill-mannered and even plebeian.[42]

Turner's sympathy with the class of his origins is illuminated by the comparison between his view of *Harewood House from the North East* and Malton's. The latter's version of Harewood is of an elegant park enjoyed by persons of culture, standing, refinement and leisure. For Turner Harewood is the domain of the working classes whose labours support the fabric of the estate. It is late evening in summer, for the sun is in the north-west, and the workers sit around enjoying a drink and picnic at the end of their day's work. The result of their efforts, a felled tree, is being carted away in front of the house and the woman who brought the refreshments makes her way home through the trees to the left. The job has been particularly hard for it has been necessary to dig out the tree roots rather than simply leave the stump, presumably for the sake of neatness, the tree being so near the front entrance of the house, and the tools of their labours, the barrow and pickaxe, lie close by. Turner's inclusion of these figures is clearly more than mere staffage. Turner marks his interest in these working people by placing them prominently in his composition and he remained interested throughout his career in the way in which the lives of working people bound them to their landscape. It was a relationship quite different from the metropolitan way of life into which he was born, and which was rapidly becoming established in industrial society at large.

9. J.M.W. Turner – ***Harewood House from the South West,*** *1797. Adopting a more distant viewpoint, and developing the human interest by including a reed-cutter and a sleeping child.*

10. J.M.W. Turner – ***Harewood House from the South East,*** *1798. Bought for 10 guineas in March 1798. In the work done for Lascelles it is possible to see Turner's emergence as a painter of landscape.*

He was always interested in the way in which such relationships were characteristic of the places he visited, and in the case of Harewood, the cultivation and management of timber has always been a central part of the life of the estate. The timber wagon passing in front of this house is heading in the direction of the timber mill at Harewood bridge, a mill which flourishes to this day.

Two more views of the house by Turner, *Harewood House from the South East* and *Harewood House from the South,* both at Harewood today (*Ills. 10, 11*), were among five drawings for which Edward the younger paid 50 guineas on 15 March 1798.[43] In the six months which separate these watercolours from the first pair, Turner had developed still further his character and identity as a painter of landscape. The house is now pushed into the distance and the subject becomes instead the grand sweep of land over the lake towards the house and the valley of the Wharfe crowned by Almscliffe Crag. In these six months Turner has attained the confidence and technique to demonstrate how such material might be brought properly within the compass of the watercolour medium. He uses opaque saturated paint, scratching-out and underwashes of bright colour to conceive the whole production in new terms for watercolour as a *painting.* The high viewpoint also enables him to exercise a trait already apparent in his pencil sketches, an endless love of observation. Throughout his life he made this devotion to observation a fundamental part of his practice. The result is some 20,000 drawings in the Turner Bequest at the Tate Gallery in London. As the sketches made at Harewood in 1797 already show, he was determined to exercise his sketching so as to extend and structure the act of looking. As anyone who has ever attempted to draw will know, there is no better device for sharpening and focusing the attention, and for making one conscious of what is being observed. The detail of Turner's drawings *(Ill. 13),* in which one feels that every field, bush, tree, pathway, road, river, stream, hill and building has not just been seen and recorded but understood, and its relationship to the whole comprehended, forms the basis of these watercolours. Such matters are perhaps taken too much for granted in an age dominated by photography, when every detail of a scene might be recorded by the unthinking press of a shutter release, but Turner in watercolours such as these was establishing to a degree never before attempted the pleasure of looking at scenery and a level of intelligent, enquiring, interested engagement with his visual experience which represents a major step forward in landscape, and which few artists have managed to attain since.

Two other pictures of the five paid for in March 1798 are compositions of *Harewood Castle*

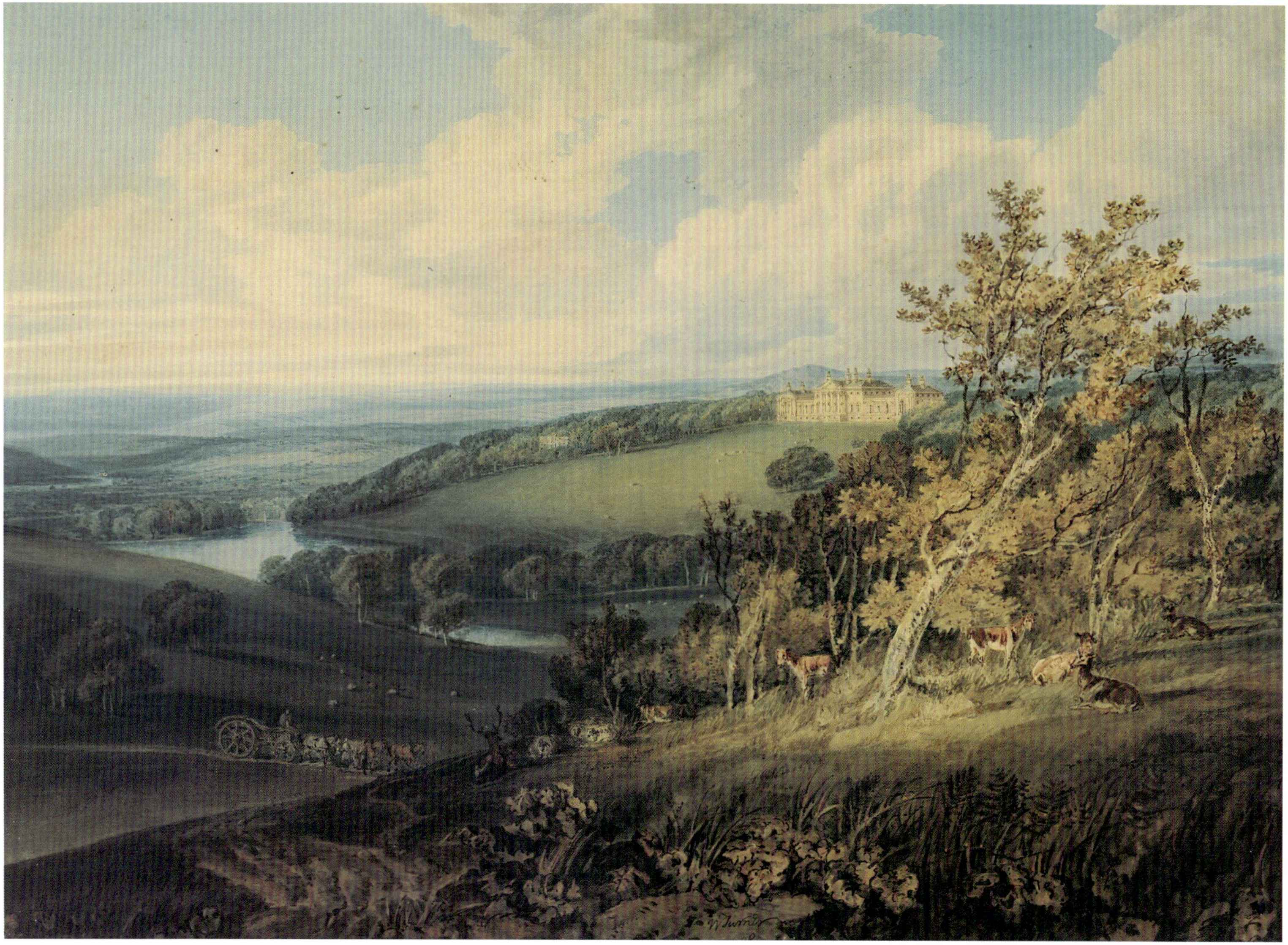

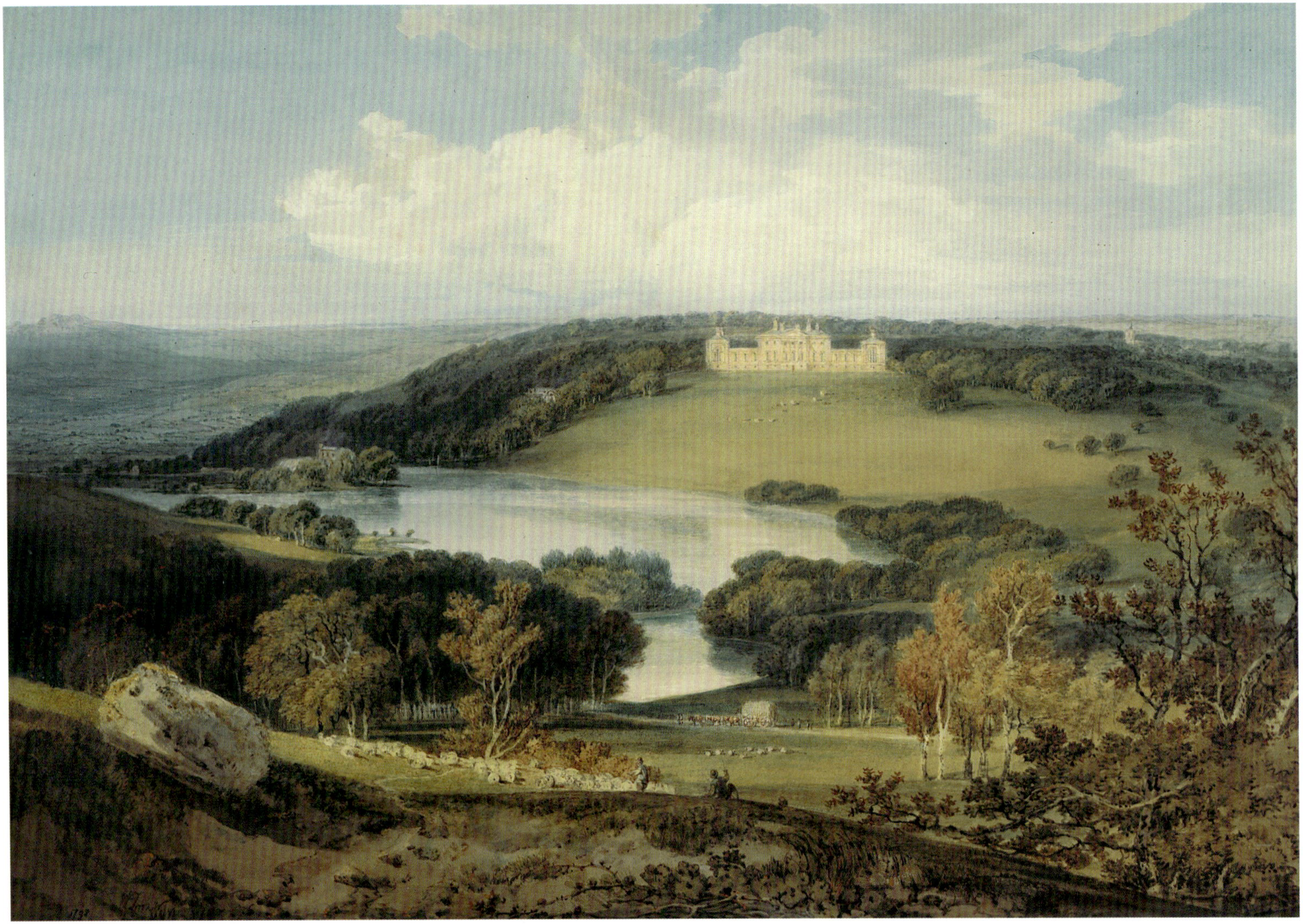

from the North and *Harewood Castle from the South East.* The first is at Harewood (*Ill.12*), but the second is in a private collection, having been given in 1858 by the 4th Earl to one of his sisters.[44] The private collection picture is nevertheless reproduced here (*Ill. 14*) since the relationship between the pair marks another major development in Turner's treatment of landscape. *Harewood Castle from the South East* shows an early summer's morning, and long shadows are cast by the sun newly risen in the north-east. The day promises to be warm and still. A woman accompanied by a child is approaching, carrying a pail upon her head, bringing milk from the farm in the valley below. A labourer with a knapsack on his back has just passed them on his way to work in the fields. In his hands he carries a long-handled tool, probably a hay-fork, for the same implement reappears in *Harewood Castle from the North* being carried away on a loaded hay wagon whilst the sun is now low in the north-west. The fork has obviously been busy since morning and new-cut hay lays in rows across the field. The day is now cooling and a wind drives up clouds from the west. Even though the shadows show that it must already be quite late, work continues on the sunlit slope below the castle. In the foreground, squalls gust through the labourers' clothes and every tree and branch appears in motion, while the haywain is hurried away to get its load under cover, and the sky grows dark, threatening rain. In this pair of pictures, Turner seems to have reconstructed the actual day he spent exploring the site, and intended that we read an interval of time between the two pictures in which work and physical experience took place which the figures in the picture and artist alike enjoyed. In the detail of the figures being gusted by the wind Turner establishes one of his central purposes, to engage with the sensations of simply being alive vitally in contact with nature. In practice Turner achieved this through his sketching, and it is worth noting that the watercolour of *Harewood Castle* in a private collection contains what seems to be a self-portrait of the artist sketching in a large leather-bound volume such as he used on his visit to Harewood in 1797.

A smaller version of *Harewood Castle from the South East* (*(Ill.15*) was brought to Harewood by the Princess Royal in the 1950s. A note in one of Turner's north of England sketchbooks of this time indicates that it was originally commissioned by a Mr Kirshaw.[45] Turner chose to make this version a rather more picturesque production than the larger version, and he changed a number of features in order to emphasise the main pictorial effects. The castle was made more decayed, its skyline more broken, the ivy was made more luxuriant, the battlements more pronounced, the window detail more emphatic. Since Mr Kirshaw could hardly have had the same familiarity with

*11. J.M.W. Turner – **Harewood House from the South,** 1798. In the details of the distant landscape Turner employs a new density of colour and exercises his characteristic love of observation.*

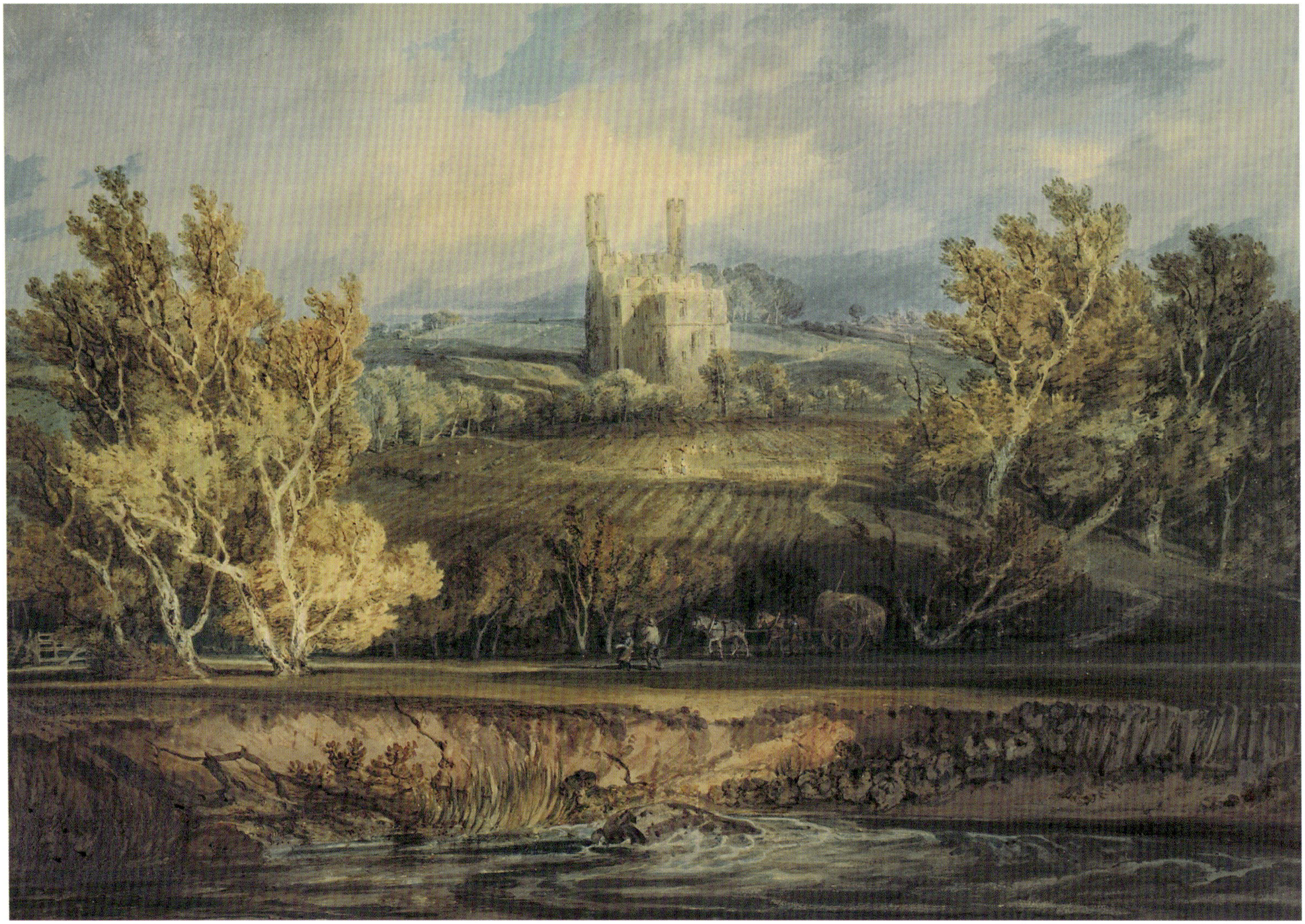

the subject as Lascelles, Turner also seems to have felt free to indulge in invention. The window above the horses, for example, has no basis in fact, sketch or larger picture, and the hood moulding above the windows to the right, together with the tracery in the middle window on the far right, are also figments of his imagination.[46] Turner's purpose was to develop the purely pictorial attributes of the subject, in particular the picturesque qualities of the ruin, the mingled tones and colours in the distance, and the dramatic leap of the eye into space when it reaches the edge of the building. The same possibilities seem to have occurred to the author of the first guidebook to Harewood published in 1819:

This beautiful ruin is nearly all covered with ivy and situated on the steep slope of a hill rising southward, on the north side of the village...the road winds gradually down the hill towards the vale of the Wharf [sic], *whose beautiful mazes may be traced to a considerable distance, which gives a softness and beauty to the scene; the eye wanders with infinite delight across a beautiful extent of country, twenty miles distant beyond York. On the other hand are prospects of unrivalled beauty, the vale itself opens to view the distant hills in Craven, the town of Otley and Otley Chiven; Farnley the beautiful seat of Walter Fawkes Esq... etc, causing an endless variety of picturesque beauties.*[47]

Turner evidently found the same 'infinite delight' in tracing the mazes of the Wharfe, and the same pleasure in detail as his eye wandered across the prospect. All of this he incorporated in his finished watercolour - the weir by the mill, the house by the bridge, every field and tree and hill, lovingly recreated over mile after mile into the distance.

12. J.M.W. Turner ***Harewood Castle from the North,*** *1798. Turner portrays a windswept landscape in which hay-cutters use the last light to finish their work in the fields.*

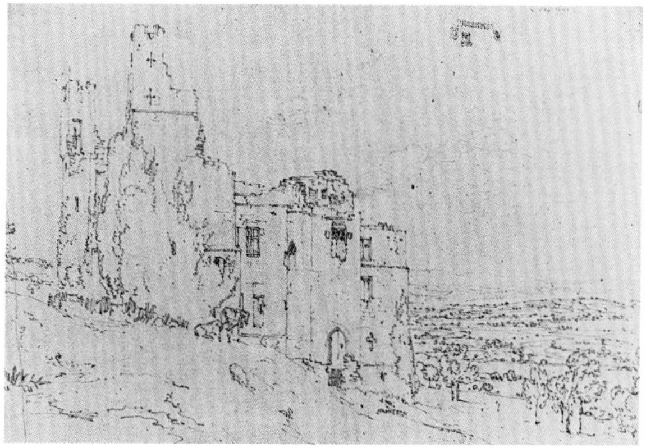

13. J.M.W. Turner – ***Harewood Castle from the South East,*** *1797. In work such as this Turner established an unrivalled sense of intelligent, enquiring, engagement with experience. (Tate Gallery, London, TB XXXIV 67)*

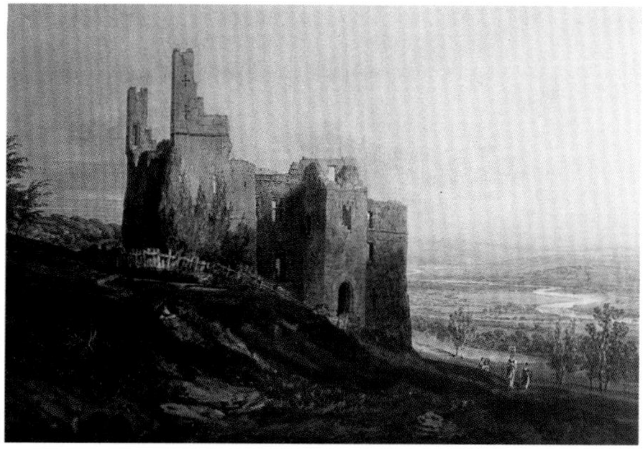

14. J.M.W. Turner – ***Harewood Castle from the South,*** *1798. The figures seem to include a self-portrait, sketching. Could his companion be Thomas Girtin? (Private Collection)*

15. J.M.W. Turner – ***Harewood Castle from the South East,*** *c.1798. A more picturesque version of the subject than the picture made for Edward Lascelles. Brought to Harewood by Princess Mary.*

If the foundations of Turner's career in landscape can be seen being laid down in the watercolours at Harewood, the tracing of its subsequent development under Lascelles' patronage will today require us to travel rather further afield. It has already been remarked that Turner's visit to Harewood in 1797 allowed him to make an extensive tour of the north of England, and it is arguable that the material he gathered on this tour allowed him to establish his national reputation through the works he afterwards exhibited at the Royal Academy.[48] Lascelles himself bought two further products of this tour, a watercolour of *Kirkstall Abbey*, now in the Fitzwilliam Museum in Cambridge, which was the fifth of the watercolours paid for in March 1798, and a larger composition of *Norham Castle*, now in the Cecil Higgins Art Gallery, Bedford, which Lascelles bought in November of the same year. In later years Lascelles completed his collection of Turner watercolours with the *Lake of Geneva, with Mt Blanc from the Lake*, now at the Yale Centre for British Art at New Haven in the United States, and *Pembroke-castle: Clearing up of a thunder-storm*, which Turner exhibited at the Royal Academy exhibition of 1806. The last major payment to Turner in the account books, which must be for one of these, is dated 8 April 1806, 'To paid Wm Turner Esq', sixty guineas.[49] The transformation in Turner's prices, from the 3 guineas which Lascelles paid for his first purchase in 1797, speaks for itself. In the interval Turner had become established as one of the greatest painters of his age.

The last documented association of Turner with Edward Lascelles is dateable to 1808 when the account books record a payment of 15 shillings for 'a book of Prints'[50] and one of Turner's sketchbooks records the commission of a watercolour of 'Fort Rock' for 60 guineas.[51] This does not seem to have come into Lascelles's collection, but seems securely identifiable with the watercolour of *Fort Roch, Val d'Aosta* which was subsequently in the collection of Walter Fawkes of Farnley Hall.[52] Fawkes's house is only four miles from Harewood, on the opposite side of the Wharfe near Otley, and this became Turner's regular resort after this time, allowing him to develop his affection for the Yorkshire scenery to which he had been first introduced by his association with Harewood. He did not altogether forget his debt to Harewood, however, and on his first visit to Farnley in 1808 he revisited his former haunt, making a series of four sketches of Harewood Castle and bridge, and a fifth of the banks of the Wharfe which stands as a touching recollection of the subjects developed in this area by his friend and associate, Thomas Girtin.[53]

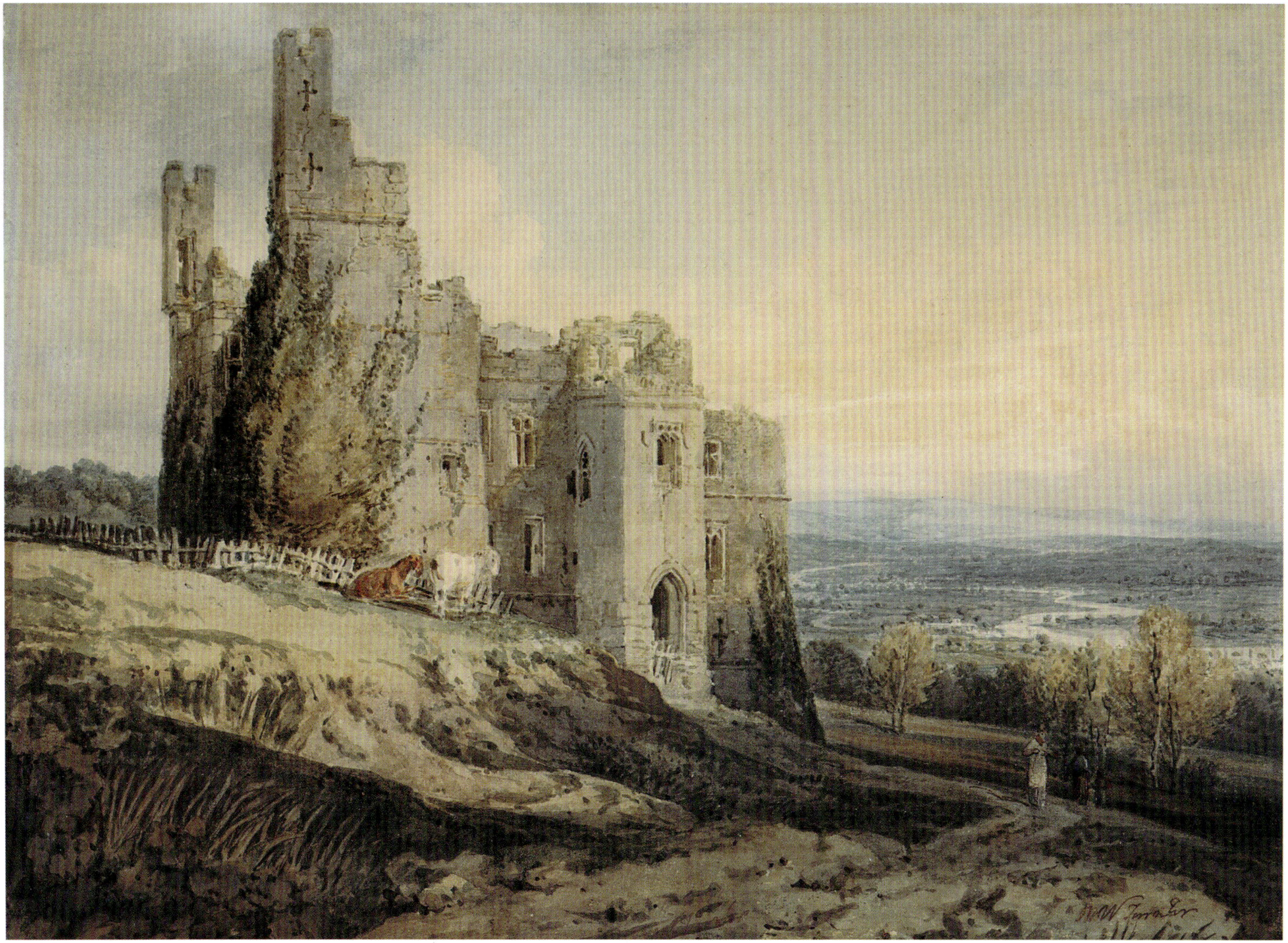

Thomas Girtin

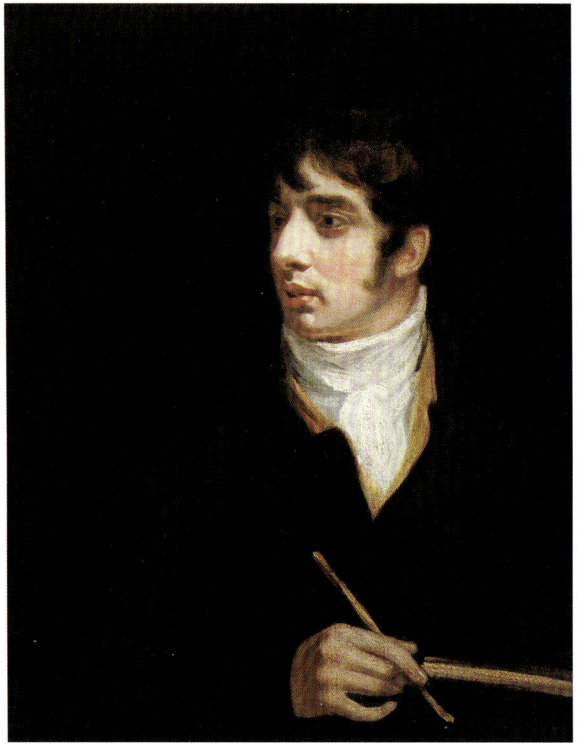

16. John Opie – ***Portrait of Thomas Girtin,*** *c.1801. Described as dashing, impulsive and bold, the same qualities can be found in much of his work. A room at Harewood was kept permanently reserved for his use. (National Portrait Gallery, London)*

LASCELLES'S PATRONAGE OF GIRTIN (*Ill. 16)* is of hardly less significance than that of Turner. For Girtin, however, the opportunity to further develop the maturity he acquired while associated with Harewood was denied by his premature death in 1802 at the age of twenty-seven, probably of consumption.[54] Turner himself trenchantly summarised what might have been: 'If Tom Girtin had lived, I should have starved'.[55]

The two artists had many similarities. They were born within weeks of one another in 1775, Girtin in February and Turner in April; within a stone's throw of one another, Girtin in Southwark, Turner on the opposite bank of the Thames in Covent Garden; and into similar social circumstances, Girtin's father being a brushmaker, Turner's a barber. They were apprenticed to artists of similar standing, Girtin to Edward Dayes and Turner to Thomas Malton, and each derived considerable instruction and influence from both. They undertook similar work as young men, colouring prints and producing work for publication, and both studied at Dr Monro's 'Academy'. They both enjoyed the early support of Viscount Malden of Cassiobury and probably through him were introduced to Edward Lascelles the younger.

Turner was certainly the more precocious of the two. Turner exhibited annually at the Royal Academy from 1790 while Girtin had to wait until 1794 before having his first work accepted. Turner exhibited oil paintings from 1796, Girtin not until his one solitary exhibit in 1801. Turner was elected Associate of the Royal Academy in 1799 at the youngest age possible of twenty-four, and was elected to the select company of only forty full Royal Academicians at the eyebrow-raising age of twenty-seven, in 1802, the year in which Girtin died. In many ways Turner has to be judged the more varied, skilled and professional of the two – in fact Girtin's drawing and technique often seems decidedly immature by comparison with work by Turner from the same time. Perhaps this slower progress is reflected in Girtin's association with Lascelles. The first payment to Girtin in the account books is dated 17 February 1798, about a year after the first payment to Turner. This might, however, lend some support to the tradition that the two artists visited Harewood together. We know that Turner's visit was in 1797, and the first payments to him for work related to that visit are dated November 1797 and March 1798, that is around the same time as the first payment to Girtin. Turner, however, was delivering major watercolours of views of Harewood at this time, but Girtin's major watercolours of Harewood subjects date from 1801. Nevertheless Girtin became Edward Lascelles's personal favourite. Their relationship was closer – on 21 November 1798 the account books record that Lascelles was informing his practice with instruction from the young artist: 'To Paid Mr Girtin for Drawings, Lessons etc...£17.17.0',[56] and one source even reports that Girtin 'had a room kept for him at Harewood House, where he lived for long periods together, and made some of his most important drawings.'[57] In 1799 when Turner was campaigning for election as Associate of the Royal Academy we hear from Farington that: 'Mr Lascelles as well as Lady Sutherland are disposed to set up Girtin against Turner who they say effects his purpose by industry – the former more genius – Turner finishes too much'.[58] In August 1800 Girtin's talents proved useful in a more practical sense, and it is recorded that he helped sketch out the effect of alterations to the landscape proposed by Humphrey Repton.[59]

In total, the collection of Edward Lascelles the younger included nineteen items by Girtin listed in the 1814 inventory (see p.57). Fourteen of these were disposed of in the 1858 sale, and a good deal of work yet remains to track all these down. The account books record payments of 5 guineas for a drawing on 17 February 1798,[60] another payment of 20 pounds for unspecified work on 9 May 1798,[61] 17 guineas on 21 November 1798 for 'Drawings, Lessons etc',[62] 32 guineas on 15 February 1799 for drawings,[63] 20 pounds on 15 January 1800 for drawings,[64] and 30 guineas on 17 February 1801 for 'several Drawings'.[65] Until we can positively identify all the work from the collection, however, it will be difficult to guess which drawings were delivered when. In addition a letter from Edward Lascelles to Girtin dated 27 June 1801 has been recorded saying: 'I hope you have made the alterations in the Drawings of this place which I wished you to do, and that you have returned them to the house in Hanover Square. I think you said they were to

17. Thomas Girtin – ***Harewood House from the South East,*** *1801. Girtin's 'genius' in full flow, sweeping the eye giddily across the composition.*

be 20 gns each. If you will call on Mr Nelson, Mect, at No.1 Hylord's Court, Crutched Friars, he will pay you on producing this letter 84 pounds. The frame-makers bill I will pay when I go to town.'[66] Ominously the same letter begins: 'I received your letter this morning, and am sorry to hear that you are under the necessity of going to another climate for the benefit of your health.' Girtin had apparently been advised to go to Madeira or the Cape of Good Hope, but in the event got no further than Paris, and then to no avail, dying on 9 November 1802 in his London studio in the Strand. He was buried at St Paul's Covent Garden on the 17th, and Turner was one of the mourners.

We are fortunate that two at least of the four drawings referred to in the letter, that is *Harewood House from the South East* and *Harewood House from the South West* have returned to Harewood (*Ills. 17, 18*).[67] The first of these, moreover, can without doubt be considered as one of Girtin's masterpieces. Furthermore, in view of the letter's reference to the frame-maker's bill, the framing and presentation of these watercolours has been, through the encouragement of Lord Harewood, a major concern for the collection at Harewood. Girtin mounted his largest drawings on wooden stretchers and traces of paint around the edges suggest that to some extent he even painted them in this state.[68] Close examination of the frames recently suggested that these were not original,[69] but we are fortunate that there is a good example of the appearance of a major collection at this time in the form of a watercolour by J.M.W. Turner of *Walter Fawkes's exhibition at Grosvenor Place, London,* dating from 1819 *(Ill. 35),* which shows a room full of Turner watercolours, all made between 1804 and 1819 in the kind of framing which the artist presumably sanctioned. This has been used as a model for those watercolours which required reframing and for their display (see p.53). Thus, apart from the all too obvious ravages of time in some cases, we can offer a rare instance of presenting the work of these artists in a manner and setting close to that which they would have intended. To modern eyes the presentation of watercolours close-framed in gilded mouldings might seem a little strange, but it was a fundamental part of the achievement of both Turner and Girtin that they developed the technical and aesthetic weight of their work to the extent that it could rival the form and *gravitas* traditionally reserved as the province of oil painting.

Girtin's view of *Harewood House from the South East* is interestingly similar in viewpoint to that painted by Turner, and also earlier by Edwin Lascelles. It seems very likely that some yardstick of Girtin's progress in relation to the more publicly

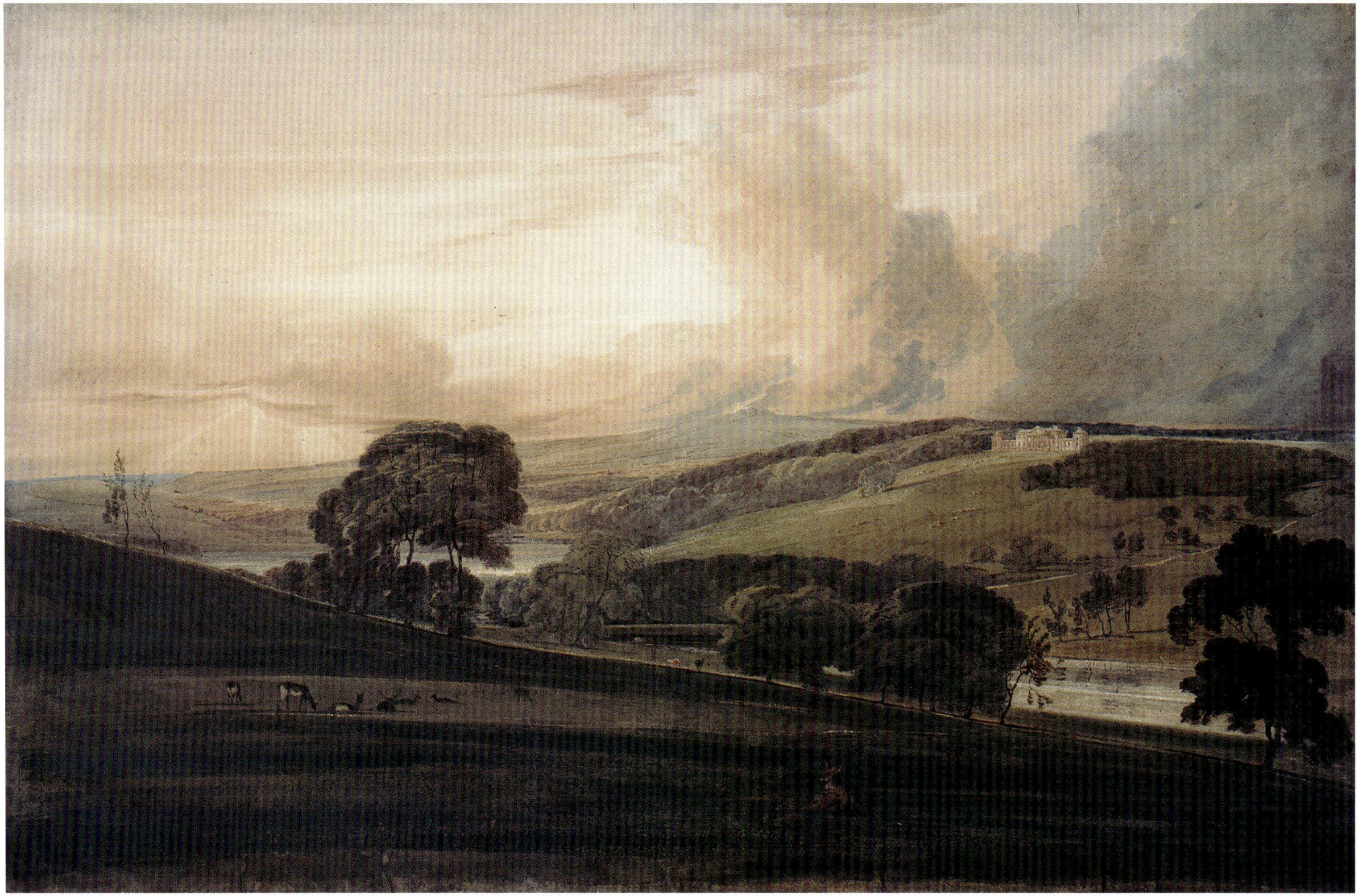

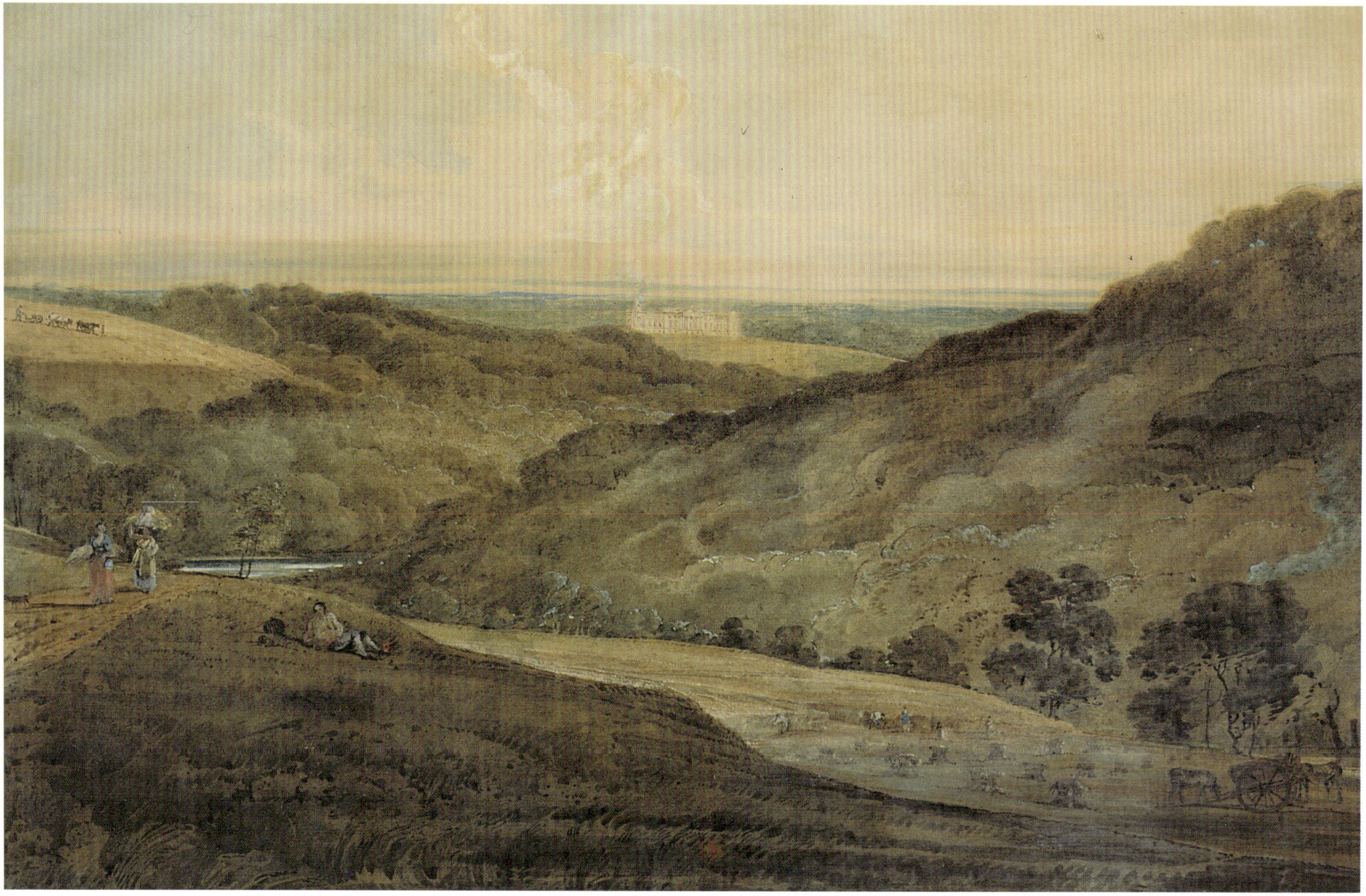

successful Turner was intended. Apart from the increased size of the Girtins over the Turners, there is a much more direct *bravura* of handling in evidence and drama of effect obtained. In comparison especially with *Harewood House from the South East* the Turners seem tranquil, contemplative, placid and content in mood, quietly surveying all before them. Girtin on the other hand attacks his subject with broad swathes of paint, bold chiaroscuro and sweeping compositional strokes. Girtin has rather less interest in observation and detail – the interest which Lascelles described as Turner's 'industry' – nor indeed, if we examine the evidence of Girtin's sketching practice (including two drawings in the Harewood collection, one of *Grimbald Bridge, Knaresborough* and the other of *Bilton Banks, near Knaresborough (Ills. 19, 20)*[70] will we find anything remotely resembling Turner's routinely careful investment of time and effort into his knowledge of his subjects. Girtin's drawings are more often brevity personified in comparison and suggest an interest in higher matters.[71] If there is any truth in the story that Turner and Girtin sketched together at Harewood this must have been in 1797, and it is tempting to speculate that the detail of the artist concentratedly sketching in Turner's large watercolour of *Harewood Castle from the South East (Ill. 14)* also includes as his companion Thomas Girtin, altogether less interested in effecting his purposes by industry.

There seems to be abundant evidence in Girtin's view of *Harewood House from the South East* of what Lascelles meant when he referred to the artist's 'genius'. The eye is given little opportunity to rest in the foreground apart from on the deer dotted around the greensward, as we are led dramatically leftward to the point of maximum contrast where the dark trees are silhouetted against the midsummer sunset and its reflection in the lake, scratched through to the sparkling white of the paper itself. From here we are swept giddily up across the front of Almscliffe Crag to the immense pile of dark cloud above the house which is seen glimmering in the sunlight against the gloom beyond. The journey is literally sensational, providing almost a roller-coaster ride for the eye across the composition, including brilliant shifts of focus from the tree to the lake and sunset which mimic an actual leap of focus from middle distance into space. Detail is sufficient to interest the eye but not to detain it from its headlong plunges and bounds, and the paintwork is bold and flooded to suggest directness of inspiration in expression.

The composition of Girtin's *Harewood House from the South West* is equally broad in its treatment, although quieter in its mood, focusing instead on a variety of harvest and ploughing incident in the foreground and middle distance,[72] including a prone young man by the road to left who might well be a self-portrait of the artist

18. Thomas Girtin – ***Harewood House from the South West,*** *1801 (detail). A tranquil composition, with details of late summer harvesting and ploughing.*

19. Thomas Girtin – ***Grimbald Bridge, near Knaresborough,*** *c.1801. Girtin used Harewood as a springboard to launch many sketching expeditions through the Yorkshire Dales. Compare Girtin's sketching style with Turner's more leisurely 'industry.'*

enjoying his observations on his visit to the estate. The matter of alterations mentioned by Lascelles in his letter is perhaps a moot point. Girtin's imaginative purposes seem to have been bought at the expense of a certain inaccuracy in the depiction of the house. In both compositions the pavilions are shown as being the same height as the main house, and the details and proportion of the building are vague throughout – one might actually say even desultory – in comparison to the care in evidence in the watercolours by Thomas Malton. In fact there are no obvious signs of any alterations having been made to either composition, and one is left to wonder whether the artist

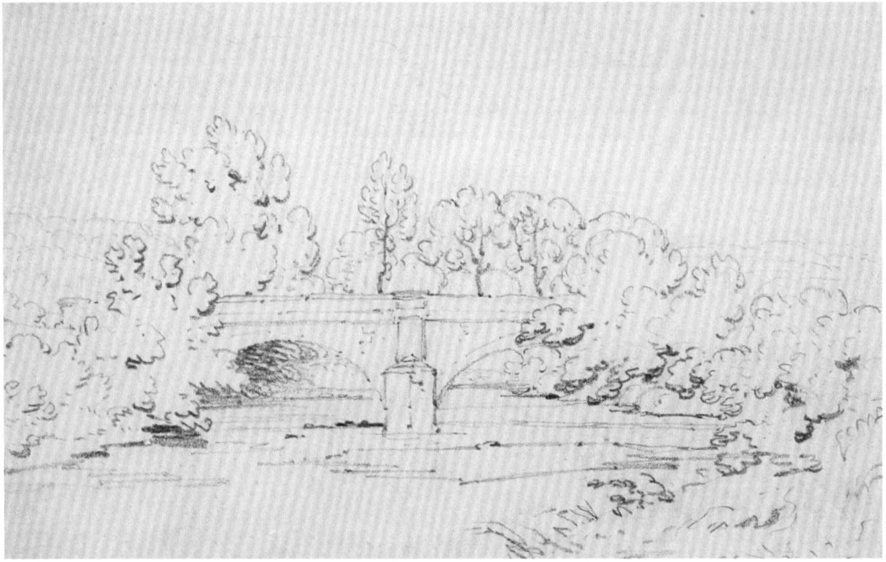

might not have been reluctant to meddle with his imaginative outpourings, having committed them so evidently cathartically to his paper.

It would be interesting to know which works by Girtin Lascelles had already acquired in 1799 when he weighed Girtin heavier than Turner in the department of genius. One possible candidate is the small watercolour of *Ships in a Harbour (Ill. 21)* which was bought by the 6th Earl of Harewood in 1937, with a provenance suggesting that it had originally formed part of the Edward Lascelles collection.[73] The Inventory of 1814 lists one subject, 'No. 60 Boats' with which it might be identified. In terms of subject matter, however, this seems to be an early work, possibly c.1795, and related to studies of Dover Harbour made by both Turner and Girtin when they were students at Dr Monro's Academy.[74] Curiously, a watercolour by Samuel Owen (1768/9 - 1857) of the same subject and composition was recently on the art market.[75] The similarity is too close to be coincidence, and both must have been made from a common source, either a previous drawing, or from the same visit. Owen's drawing is the more mature of the two and makes the Girtin seem extremely tentative. Girtin's treatment of the boat to the left seems particularly juvenile, and one might suspect that this is a work which must predate by some years the first reference to Girtin in the account books of 1798. Nevertheless the picture shows some signs of Girtin's emerging talents. The two men caulking the side of the boat to the left, dangling against the light of the sails behind, is a dramatic touch. The watercolour also takes some steps towards a manner of painting associated particularly with Girtin, at least in his smaller work, using softly modulated colour applied more obviously wetly than was usually the case and touched with blobs and highlights of bright colour. This style of handling itself constituted a breakthrough for the handling of the medium. Girtin is allowing the formal properties of the paint - its *facture* - to assert itself, and to become an integral part of the finished product. In his own way Girtin, like Turner, asserted distinctively the fact of his work being in watercolour, and made a visible aesthetic feature of that fact. In his mature work this resulted in a unique equation of style and subject-matter, and the achievement of abstract formal harmony, which had a profound influence on the generation of watercolourists which followed him.

There is one interesting example of Girtin's radically simplified style in the Harewood Collection, *An Estuary Scene, probably in Devon (Ill. 22),* dating from c.1801.[76] The watercolour has remained in the Harewood collection since its purchase by Edward Lascelles[77], and seems to survive to us in its original frame, the drawing having been stuck down on a backing sheet with a couple of faint ruled pencil lines to separate it from the shadows that might be cast by the edge of the moulding. Although the picture is sadly faded, the sky being completely drained of any colour, enough survives to suggest the expansiveness and serenity of which Girtin was capable. Even in its present condition a strong sense of artistic personality is conveyed, and those viewers with sharp eyesight will notice that there is also a sign of his physical presence in the painting. In the water just below the seated cow, Girtin has left his fingerprint, his fingertip, as artists' fingertips are perhaps wont to be, having been covered in the brown paint he was using at the time.

20. Thomas Girtin – ***Bilton Banks, near Knaresborough,*** *c.1801. A view on the river Nidd, about a mile upstream of Knaresborough.*

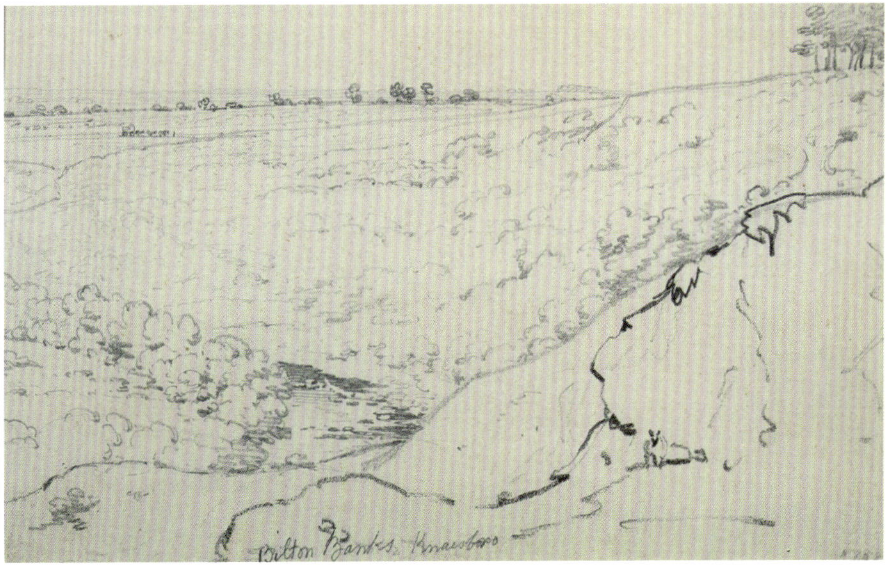

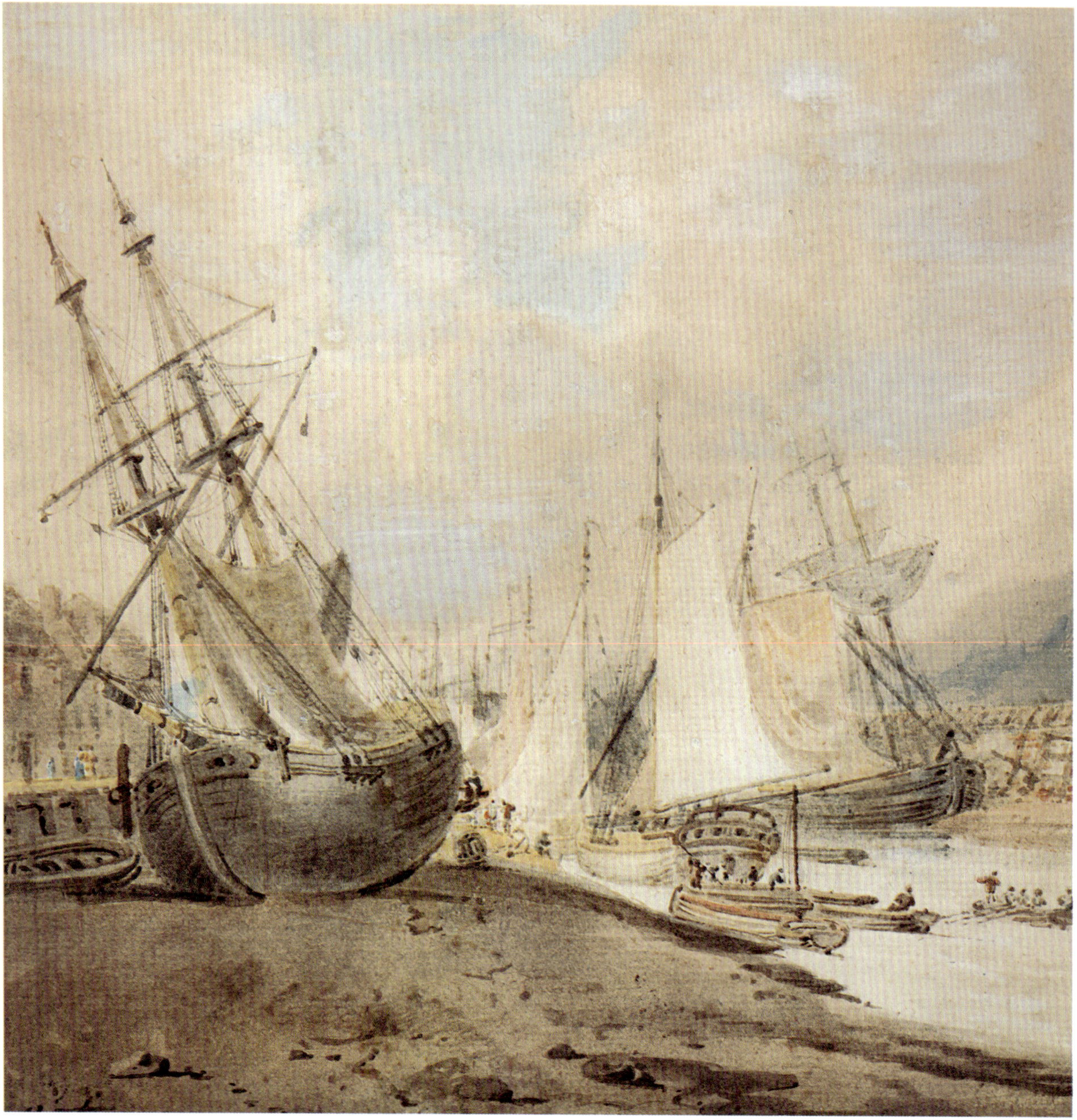

21. Thomas Girtin – ***Ships in a Harbour,*** *c.1795. An early work, but showing Girtin's characteristic fluid handling, and a typically dramatic detail of the two figures caulking the ship, silhouetted against the sails beyond.*

For Girtin, like Turner, Harewood was important also for the springboard it offered to launch sketching expeditions through Yorkshire and the north of England. Although Turner seems only to have visited Harewood House once in 1797, the opportunity to sketch in the north of England was crucially important to his development. John Ruskin claimed that it 'first opened to him the joy, and love of his life'.[78] Perhaps even more so for Girtin, north of England scenery was the most important source of subject matter. He made his first tour north in 1796, but we do not know whether he visited Harewood on that occasion, but thereafter he seems to have journeyed north regularly, and tours of 1799, 1800 and 1801 have been identified.[79] The Harewood collection contains one important example of his Yorkshire work, a view of *York Minster from the*

22. Thomas Girtin – ***An Estuary Scene, probably in Devon,*** *c.1801. Note Girtin's fingerprint in the water below the cow.*

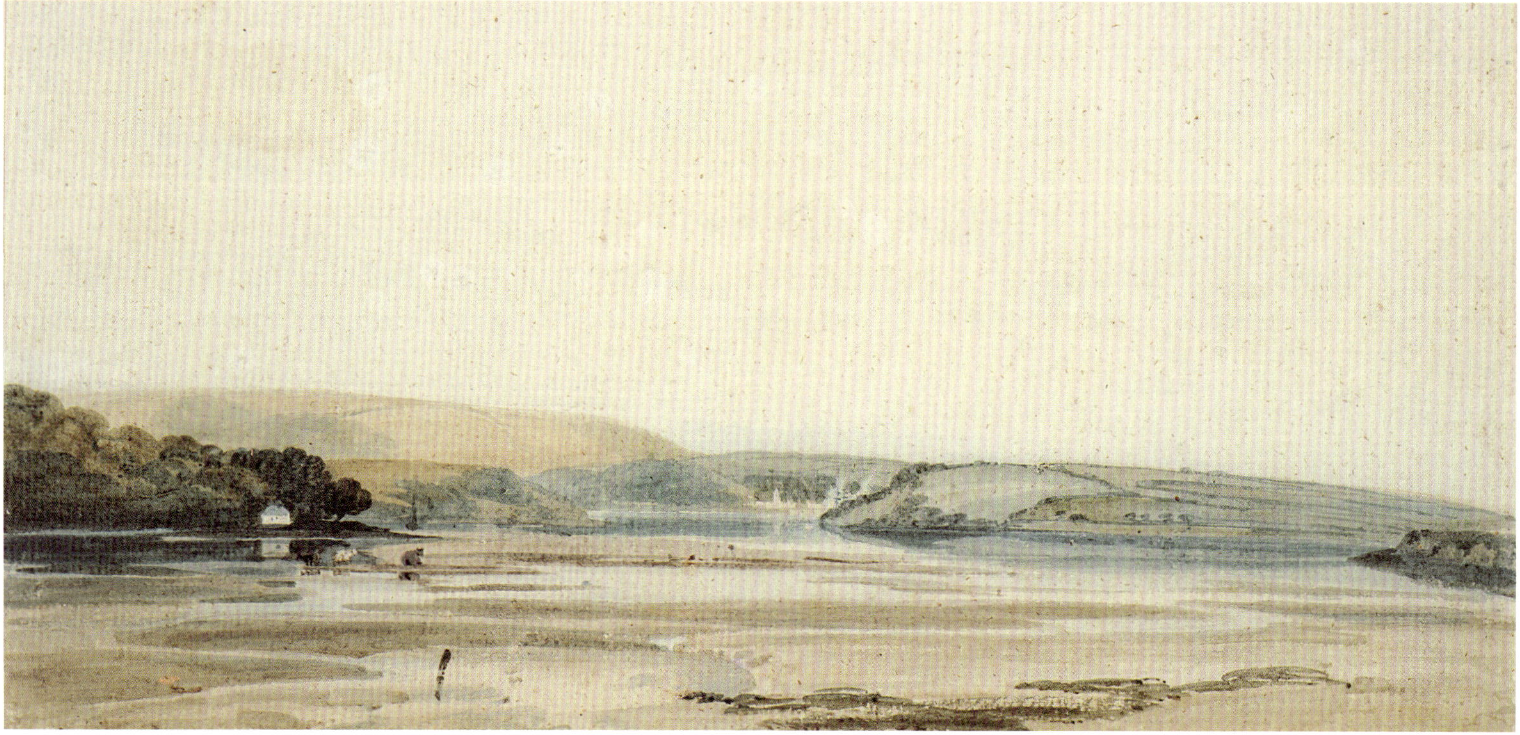

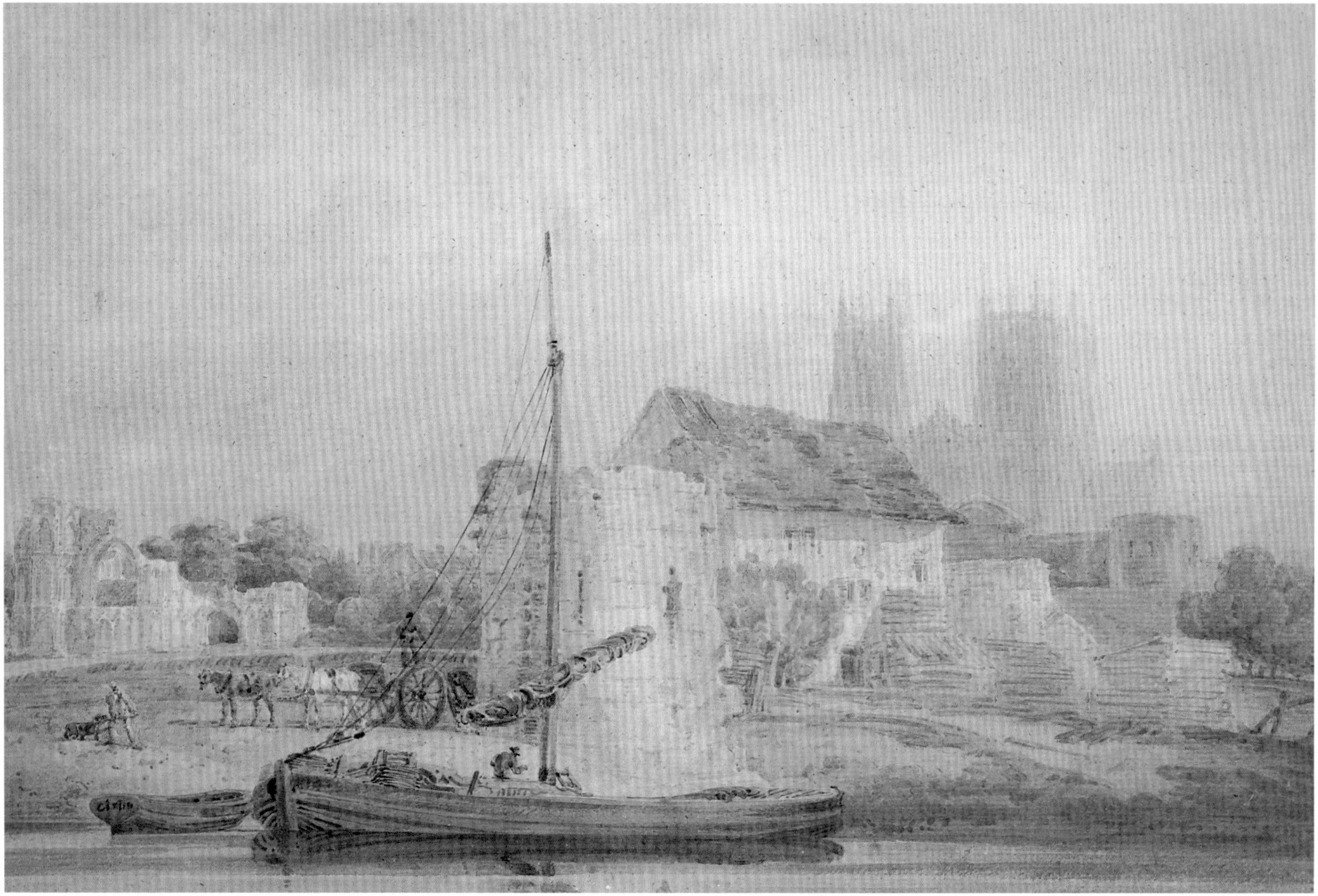

River Ouse (Ill. 23), recording the view looking over the river to the grounds of St Mary's Abbey, with the abbey ruins to the left, St Mary's tower in the centre and the fourteenth century Hospitium to the right. The watercolour was bought by the 6th Earl probably in the 1930s and, although not part of Edward Lascelles's original collection, it nevertheless represents an excellent example of the kind of work that Girtin's visits to the north enabled him to make.[80] Once again it might be observed that the drawing is in places a little inept. The foreground boat, for example, is less than convincing, and the form of the woodsheds to the right is rather hard to read. Despite the fact that the watercolour is now rather faded, it is nevertheless impressive in the way in which the whole is bound together by a delicate skein of dappled colour. It might further be contended that Girtin identifies himself, like Turner, with the world of his class – on the working shores of the river, surrounded by the modest buildings and appurtenances of the world of work, rather than with the grand world represented by the Minster in the background. In this respect it might be significant that Turner sketched exactly the same subject, with an equal emphasis on the foreground working environment, from almost exactly the same viewpoint, on his visit to York in 1797.[81]

Perhaps one of Girtin's greatest artistic successes in these terms is the watercolour of *Harewood Bridge (Ill. 24)* at Harewood which Edward Lascelles bought probably in 1801.[82] The viewpoint itself is somewhat obscure, the artist finding himself at what must have been a little-visited spot immediately downstream of the bridge on the south bank. The picture is almost monochromatic, with the large mass of the bridge at the left only just balanced by the cottages on the opposite bank and the sweep of the river across the weir. Into this Girtin has introduced one of his most extraordinary figure compositions. A group of labourers is perched precariously on planking in the middle of the river, hauling on a multi-stranded rope, to drive a pile into the bed of the river. Evidently some repairs to the weir are being made. Immediately to the left, two men supervise the operation, one leaning forward to appraise the progress being made, while on the far left a mason holds up a sight stick to make sure that the pile remains vertical. The lifting gear makes a striking sight perched as it is between the masses of masonry around, and over the flow of water beneath, and the introduction of the mason and the crouching foreman reminds us of the process of visual judgement in which we, the workers and the artist are all engaged.

The composition turns around the flow of the river from left to right, and this is mirrored by the flow of the clouds above. Against this constant dynamic, the bridge and the endeavours of the

*23. Thomas Girtin – **York Minster from the River Ouse**, c.1800. With St Mary's Abbey to the left, and the fourteenth century Hospitium to the right, then in use as a boatyard.*

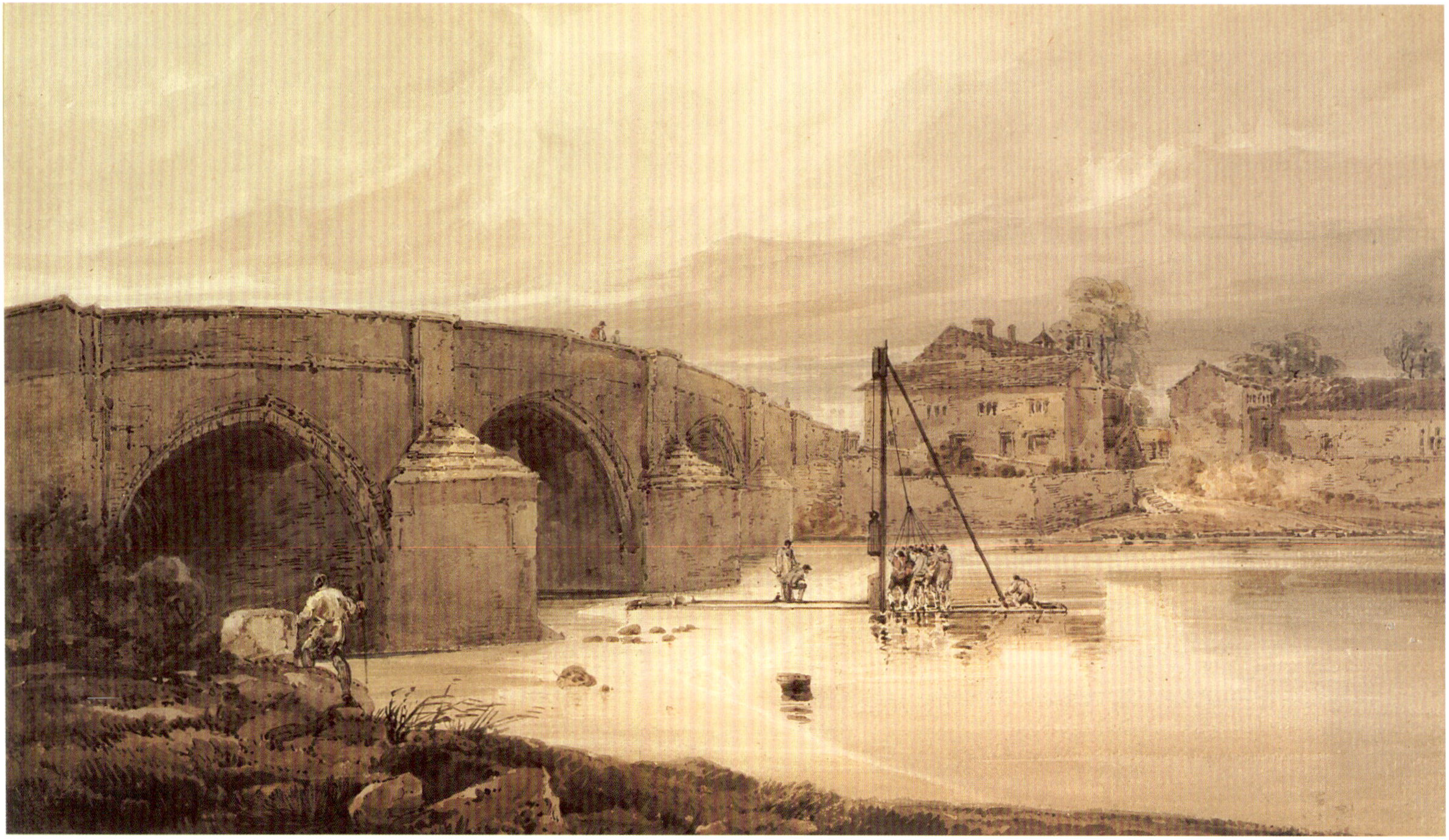

24. Thomas Girtin –
***Harewood Bridge,** c.1801.*
Undoubtedly one of Girtin's most elemental masterpieces. The treatment of the figures and reflections is particularly brilliant.

labourers take on an almost heroic dimension, symbolic of human attempts to create something steadfast against the flow of time. The elemental aspects of these efforts are further reinforced by the limited palette, eschewing anything decorative or superfluous for the essential and profound. It is striking that Girtin found such things in an obscure viewpoint and with such mundane labouring activities. It is, however, a characteristic of much of his work that he ignores the features of sites which normally attracted attention, and selects material that most others would not have deemed worthy of consideration. *Harewood Bridge* represents an important facet of Girtin's 'genius', his capacity to find profundity in 'ordinary' matter. It is almost as if the whole purpose of this endeavour on the river is to construct an harmonious aesthetic whole, an abstract significance of lines, tone, form and mass, made of masonry and flowing water. As if to emphasise that, in making out the figures hauling on the rope Girtin has deployed some of the most brilliant and deft passages of paintwork to be found anywhere in his work, and finally introduced two figures on the bridge, who stop, like us, to discover unexpected interest in what they find before them.

Girtin had an extraordinary influence on the young artists around him, particularly with respect to his development of the abstract aesthetics of watercolour, his tendency to simplification, and his selection of quiet corners of nature on which to meditate. This had a particularly profound influence on John Sell Cotman, who

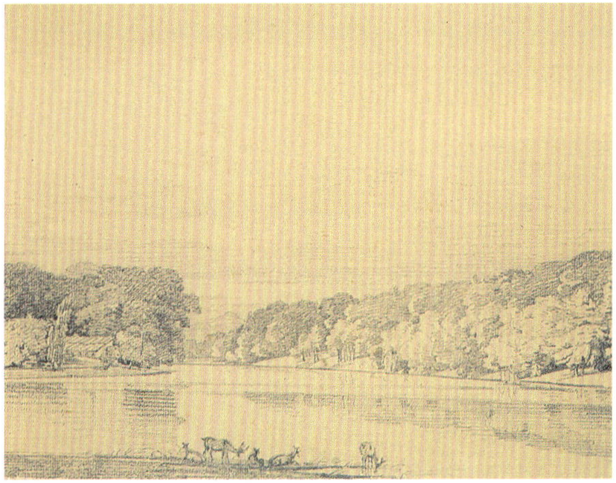

25. Attributed to John Sell Cotman – ***Harewood Lake, with Almscliffe Crag in the distance,*** *c.1803. Formerly attributed to Edward Lascelles, but far too accomplished to be anything other than the work of a professional artist.*

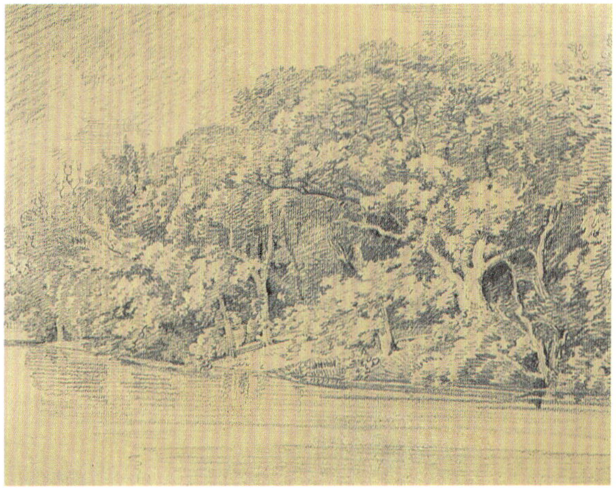

26. Attributed to John Sell Cotman – ***Trees by Harewood Lake,*** *c.1803. The intensity of the pencil work closely resembles that of Cotman.*

*27. Attributed to John Sell Cotman – **Harewood House from the South East,** c.1803.*

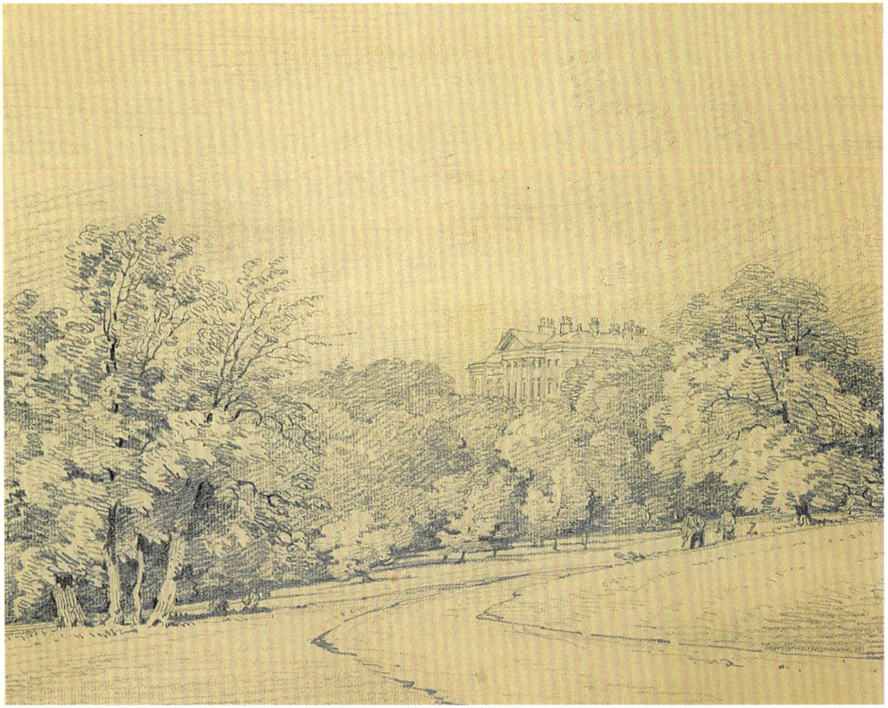

was born in 1782, moved to London about 1798, and immediately became involved in Girtin's circle. In 1803 he visited Yorkshire and in subsequent visits in 1804 and 1805 made some of the most extraordinarily beautiful watercolours ever painted.[83] We know that he had some association with Edward Lascelles for the Inventory records two compositions in the collection in 1814.[84] Hitherto no other connection between Harewood and Cotman has been established, but there are three pencil drawings in the Harewood collection (*Ills. 25, 26, 27*) which the present author is inclined to suspect might be his work, or that of a close contemporary.[85] These were formerly attributed to Edward Lascelles, but do not compare at all with the known work in the album at Harewood (*Ill. 5*). These drawings are far too accomplished to be anything other than the work of an extremely talented professional artist. The command of tone and quality of mark making is closely paralleled by many drawings by Cotman of this period, particularly in respect of the negative spaces left by areas of dark tone.[86] The most remarkable feature of the Harewood drawings is the intensity of the work, and the variety of marks that the artist brought to bear on his undemonstrative subjects around the lake. It is the same quality of meditative transcendence which Cotman achieved in the Yorkshire masterpieces of about 1805.

John Varley

The last important group of works from Edward Lascelles's collection to survive at Harewood is by an artist slightly younger than Turner and Girtin. John Varley (*Ill. 28*) was born in 1778, and also enjoyed humble origins, his family being impoverished following his father's death in 1791.[87] 'Poor Varley', it was reported by one of his friends, 'began the world with tattered clothes and shoes tied with string to keep them on... He rose early, drew until it was time to attend his situation, and set off with a large ragged portfolio, and a string over his shoulder attached to it... So great an enthusiast I never in the whole of my long practice beheld.'[88] He seems to have been quite a character, Herculean in strength but entertainingly deficient in its application, and blessed with a gregarious and careless nature. He socialised with incautious generosity and although professionally successful, exhibiting over 700 works in his life and making, it is estimated, ten times that number in total, working fourteen hours a day for forty years, he was always in debt. He seems to have thought something amiss if he failed to be arrested less than once or twice every month, and sailed through his troubles with blithe optimism, and by producing a great deal of work to keep his creditors at bay. Around the late 1790s, he too was employed in the society of Dr Monro's Academy, and possibly through this, like Turner and Girtin, came into the circle of the Earl of Essex and Edward Lascelles.

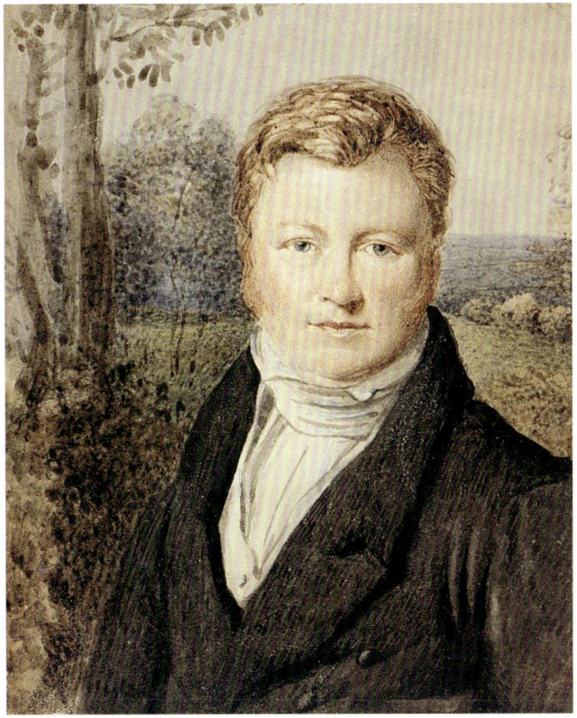

*28. John Linnell – **Portrait of John Varley**, c.1810. Varley was a generous-hearted and gregarious character, always in debt, and admired by a wide circle of fellow-water-colourists. (Courtesy of the Trustees of the Victoria and Albert Museum, London)*

There is only one payment to him in the account books, that dated 16 March 1801 for 15 guineas for a drawing.[89] He visited Yorkshire in 1803[90] and presumably visited Harewood then, since water-colours at the house are dated to that year. The 1814 Inventory lists six works in the collection, four views of Harewood House, one view of Harewood Castle, and a view of Snowdon. The Harewood subjects remain in the Harewood collection, including two large views of the house

*29. John Varley – **Harewood House from the North West,** 1803. Varley's work at Harewood represents one of his most important early commissions. The five children seen here might be the four sons and eldest daughter of Henry Lascelles, later 2nd Earl, then aged between one and seven.*

from the north-west and south- west (*Ills. 29, 30)*, two slightly smaller views, one of the house from the south-east and another of Harewood Castle (*Ills. 31, 32*), together with two further views of the house from the south-east which are unfortunately too faded to be exhibitable.[91]

The two large watercolours of *Harewood House from the North West* (*Ill.29*) and *Harewood House from the South West* (*Ill. 30*) must be considered as some of his most important early work. They represent one of the most important commissions of his career to date, and demonstrate the utmost of his capabilities at this time. At first sight, apart from their size, they resemble the earlier watercolours by Malton in the care with which the architectural detail of the house has been treated. The general composition also resembles eighteenth century approaches, together with the tasteful and reticent colouring.[92] Even at this time, however, Varley was known for the ingenuity of his method, and at a meeting in 1802 Farington recorded that 'Much was said about the singularities of Varley, an ingenious young man who had been making drawings in Wales'.[93] The Harewood watercolours certainly reward close scrutiny, especially in the treatment of the trees in the middle distance and the details of the house. The former involve a quite brilliant use of stopping-out fluid - a process whereby the painter could apply a waterproof substance to the paper which would resist the wash, and which might then be removed to allow further work over the untouched areas – and also a wonderfully sensitive use of a restricted range of colour which is reminiscent of Cotman at his best. In the treatment of the architecture the windows are particularly noteworthy, with beautifully controlled panes of colour cloisonnéed one next to the other. In *Harewood House from the North West* the green railings act particularly well as a colour foil for the rest of the composition and in *Harewood House from the South West* Varley bravely shows the left half of the house caught in sunlight whilst the right side is plunged into cool shade, suggesting the passing of a cloud, and the instantaneousness of the moment captured.

The figures are also worth studying closely. In *Harewood House from the North West* a figure on the steps gives scale to the whole house, while in the right foreground two ladies are entertaining a clutch of five young children to pony rides on the lawn. One of the children plays with a spaniel. The boys are dressed in striking blue sailor suits and three of the children we can see have red hair, and we might suspect that the group had some origin in Varley's observations on his visit to Harewood, especially since the little girl in *Harewood House from the South West* also has red hair and is attended by a similar dog to that seen on the front lawn. There were indeed five young

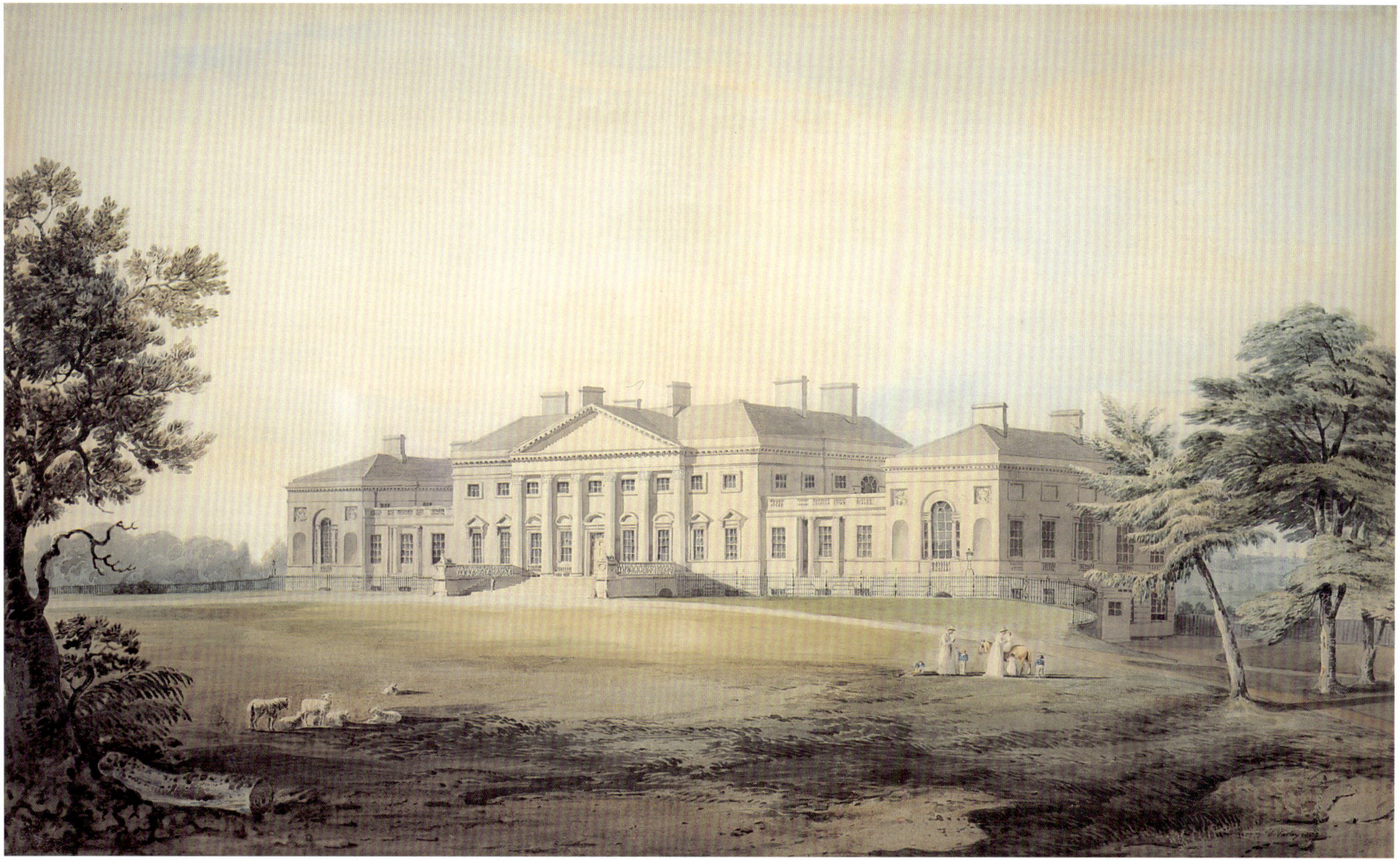

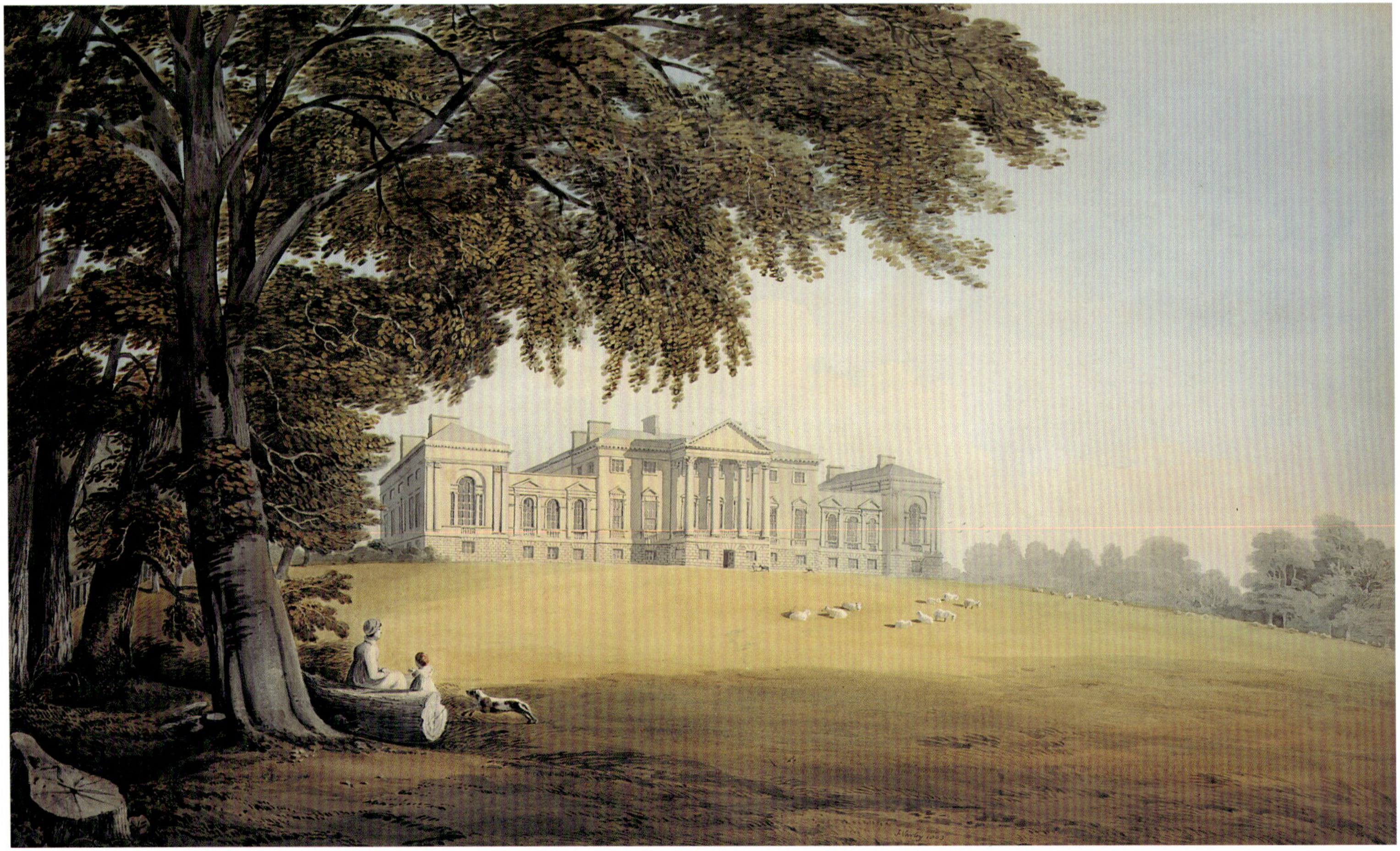

children at Harewood in 1803. Henry Lascelles, younger brother of Edward the younger, who later became 2nd Earl on the death of his father in 1820, had married in 1794. The first of his children, another Edward, was born in 1796, and he was followed in rapid succession by Henry in 1797, William in 1798, Edwin in 1799 and Harriet in 1802. Harewood must have been a lively place with five children aged between seven and one in the house, and the children would certainly have required considerable entertainment. Furthermore their mother, Henrietta, as revealed in the portrait of her by Hoppner at Harewood[94] had brilliant auburn locks, and it is tempting to surmise that she passed this characteristic to her children at least while they were

*30. John Varley – **Harewood House from the South West,** 1803. A boy appears to be attempting to persuade a donkey into the basement of the house. Note that the side of the house is in sunlight, while the right is in shade, suggesting a passing cloud and an instantaneous moment.*

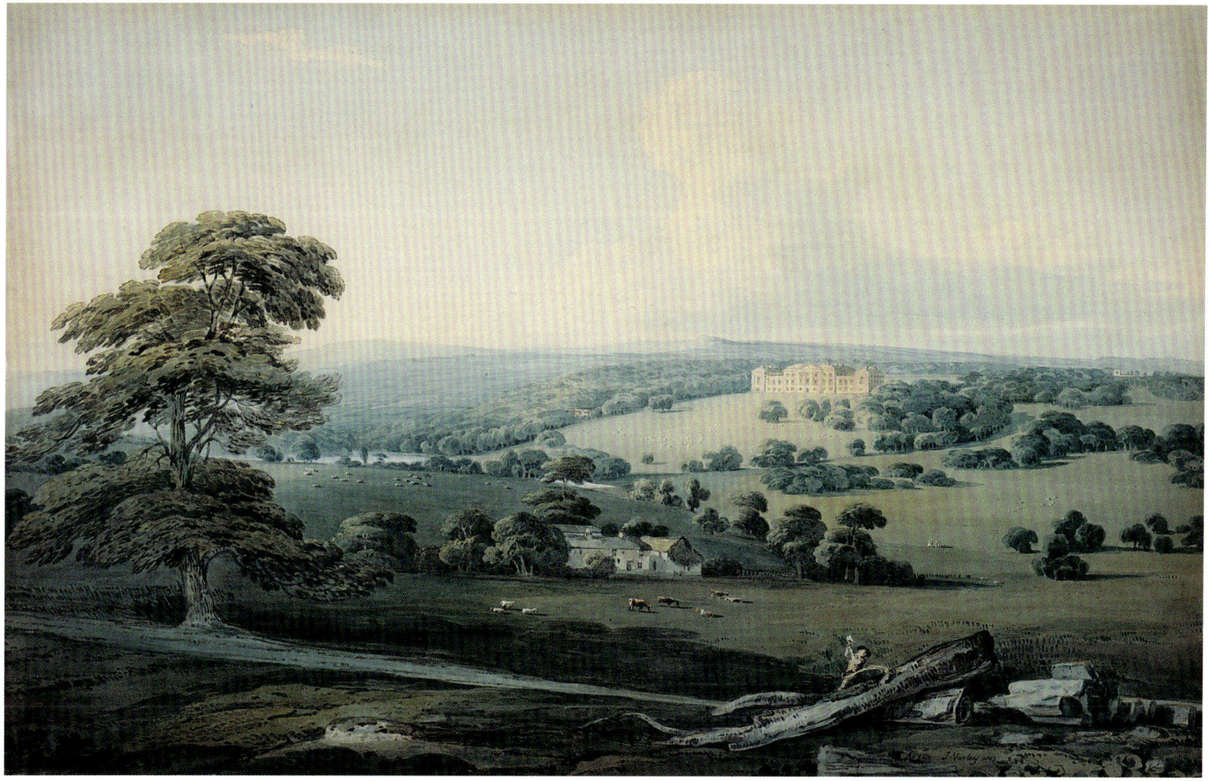

*31. John Varley – **Harewood House from the South East,** 1803. Compare the earlier views by Edward Lascelles, Turner and Girtin.*

young, and that the woman seated in Varley's view of *Harewood House from the South West* might well be Henrietta accompanied by her daughter Harriet, then a toddler just past her first birthday. It might also be noted that in the same south view there is a rather curious detail of a figure, no doubt one of the boys, apparently encouraging two donkeys into the basement entrance of the house.[95]

In the same year Varley also painted a pair of Harewood landscapes, a *View of Harewood House from the South East* (*Ill. 31*) and a view of *Harewood Castle from the West* (*Ill. 32*). The last is a relatively recent acquisition by the present Lord Harewood.[96] One wonders whether Varley might not have had the opportunity to study Turner's 1797-8 watercolours, for both of his works show an attempt to infuse similar solidity of colouring, similar interest in the delineation of distant fields, hedgerows and trees, and similar foreground incident. *Harewood House from the South East* provides a direct measure of his own ability since the subject had already been tackled by Edwin Lascelles, Turner and Girtin.[97] Though one cannot perhaps make the same aesthetic claims for Varley's work as for Turner's or Girtin's, it nevertheless demonstrates the ambition and weight which watercolourists were aspiring to in the early years of the nineteenth century. Furthermore Varley was close to the heart of the group which was driving these ambitions along. He was a member of the Sketching Society, an informal group of young watercolourists which Girtin had founded in 1799, and attended meetings with John Sell Cotman in the years immediately following Girtin's death.[98] In 1804, the year after these large Harewood subjects were painted, he was a founder-member of the Society of Painters in Watercolour which in many ways represented the public apotheosis of the medium, establishing its own exhibition space and a professional grouping of artists who wished to be particularly identified with the medium as a newly established

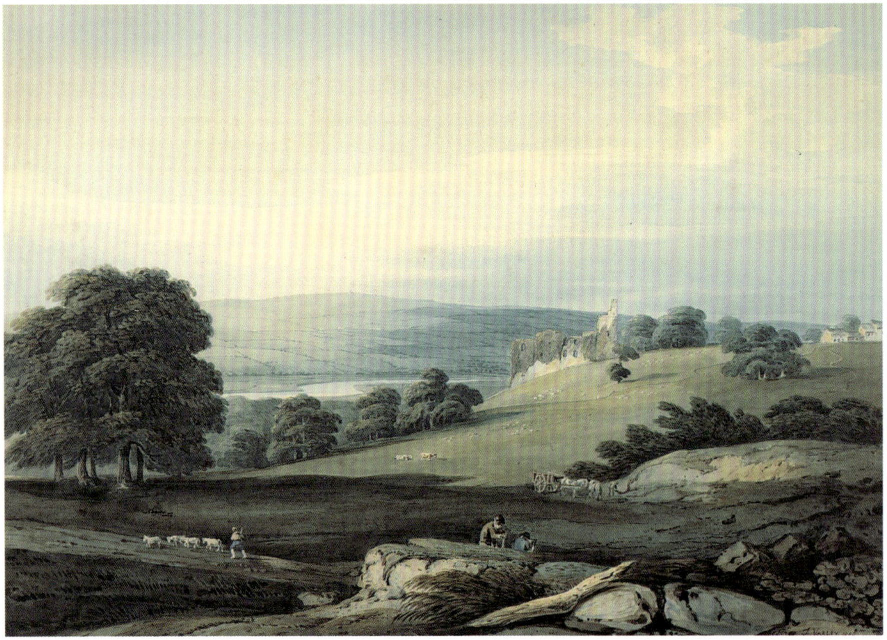

32. John Varley – ***Harewood Castle from the West,*** *1803. Varley was close to the heart of the revolution in English watercolour, and his work was widely influential on the generation that followed him.*

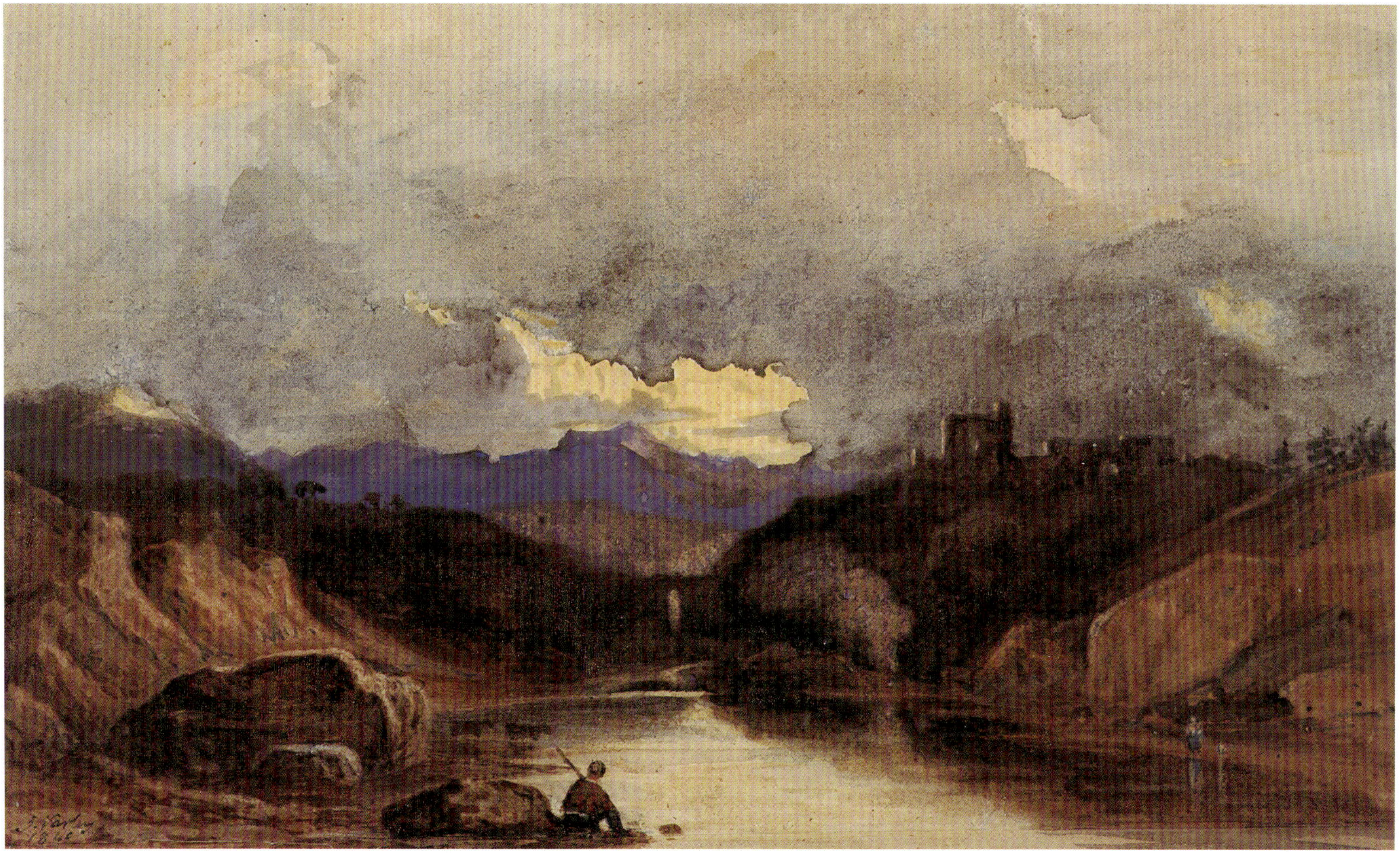

33. John Varley –
Twilight after a storm,
1840. Varley's later work has a visionary richness very like that of his close friend Samuel Palmer.

distinctive and independent practice. Varley went on to enjoy a long and prolific career as painter and teacher, and through his publications, to become a widely read and influential theorist of the practice of landscape in watercolour.[99] His circle of friends, pupils and admirers included William Blake, John Linnell, William Mulready, William Henry Hunt, Francis Oliver Finch, William Turner of Oxford, Samuel Palmer, David Cox, Peter de Wint and Anthony Vandyck Copley Fielding. In this context it is interesting that two watercolours by Varley bequeathed to the 6th Earl of Harewood, *Twilight after a storm* (*Ill. 33*), dated 1840, and *Landscape with figures* (*Ill. 34*), dating from 1841, the last year of his life, have similarities to the work of Samuel Palmer, attaining an almost visionary richness, accentuated by a richly worked, highly gummed surface and the use of washes of orange, purple and brown on a jewel-like scale.[100]

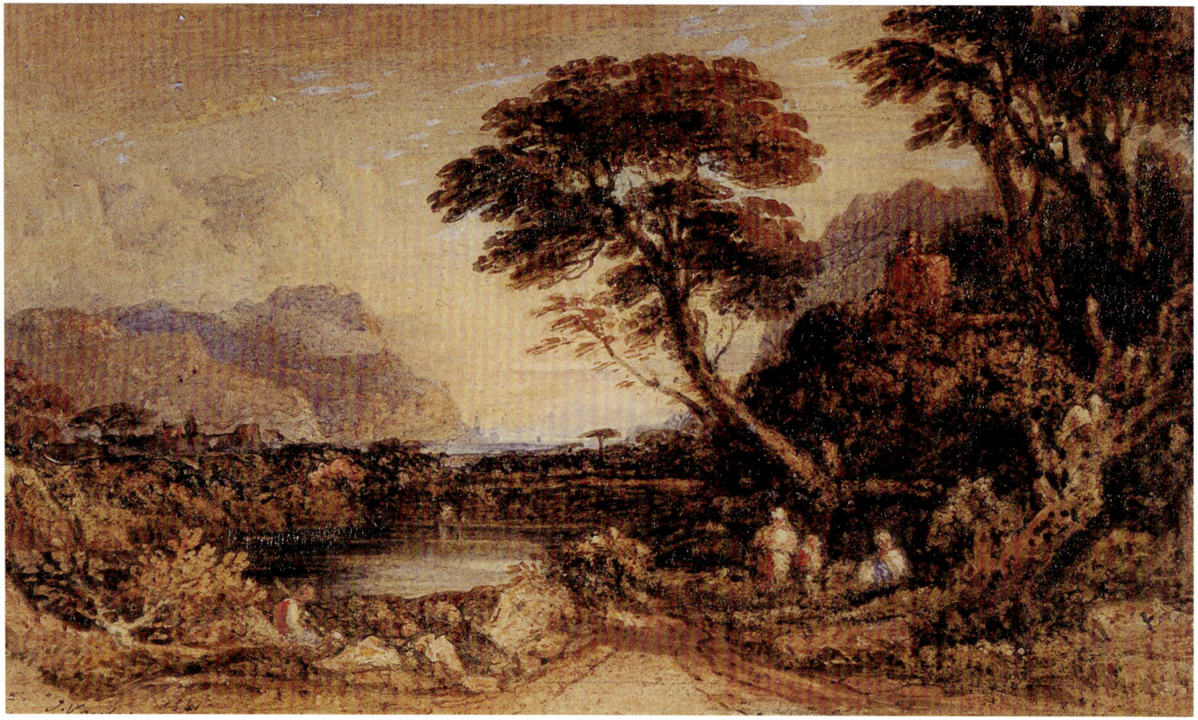

34. John Varley – ***Landscape with figures,*** *1841. Painted in the last year of his life.*

Later History and Acquisitions

EDWARD LASCELLES'S collection also contained work by Augustus Wall Callcott, Peter de Wint and William Havell, all major artists of the generation immediately following that of Girtin and Turner. Many of their works fetched high prices at the 1858 sale,[101] and some must have been major pieces. It is hoped that further research will be able to paint a much more detailed picture of the association of these artists with Lascelles. In the meantime we must wonder what prompted the 4th Earl to dispose of the collection. Certainly the sale followed precipitously on his inheriting the title in 1857. It seems possible that this was something to do with the fragility of watercolours and their susceptibility to light. As one historian put it: 'It subsequently was feared that watercolours inevitably must fade into invisibility [and] nearly the whole of the collection was sold by auction at Christie's.[102] Some of the works which survive to us have been badly faded by exposure to sunlight, and since this was not so well understood at the time they were made, or during the first half of the nineteenth century, it is highly likely that signs of damage were already beginning to appear in 1857. The Turners of Harewood subjects were mostly given to members of the family, and the remainder of the collection went under the hammer on 1 May 1858. It has been the task of later generations of the family to bring back to Harewood as much of the collection as has been possible, and to acquire numerous other examples of Harewood's association with the watercolour tradition.

Turner's *Harewood House from the North East* and *Harewood House from the South West* were quite quickly returned to Harewood, being bequeathed by the 4th Earl's sisters to whom they had been given, to the 5th Earl in the 1880s, and Turner's *Harewood House from the South East* was given to the 6th Earl and Princess Mary by the Countess of Wharncliffe as a wedding present in 1922. The 6th Earl and Princess Mary were responsible for most of the major acquisitions and reacquisitions of watercolours, along with the major collection of old masters that can also be seen at Harewood, over a long period from about 1919 up until the 1950s. Princess Mary was particularly fond of watercolours, and from the 1930s her Sitting-room at Harewood was the home of most of the collection. In this situation the watercolours survived very well, for many of them remain in fresh condition. In recent years George, 7th Earl of Harewood, has maintained the Harewood connection with watercolour and has continued work on the reacquisition of watercolours from Edward Lascelles's collection including John Varley's *Harewood House from the South East* and *Harewood Castle*, and has also acquired other notable examples associated with Harewood including John Scarlett Davis's watercolour of *The Gallery at Harewood* and, most recently, Francis Stevens's watercolour of *Harewood House from the South (Ill. 35).* In 1992 Princess Mary's Sitting-room was restored to its original appearance as a bedroom, and the reorganisation thus gave the opportunity to provide a new home for the watercolours in the East wing. With the 7th Earl's guidance and encouragement the watercolours have been restored to frames in accord with their historical context and can now be displayed in a setting reminiscent of the environment for which they were originally designed, but with modern environmental and lighting controls, and hung in such a way that the visitor will be able to examine them on closer and more intimate terms. Under these conditions it is hoped that visitors will be able to enjoy the fruits of Harewood's association with watercolour in conditions appropriate to the seminal role of the house in the development of the medium.

35. Francis Stevens – ***Harewood House from the South,*** *c.1817.*

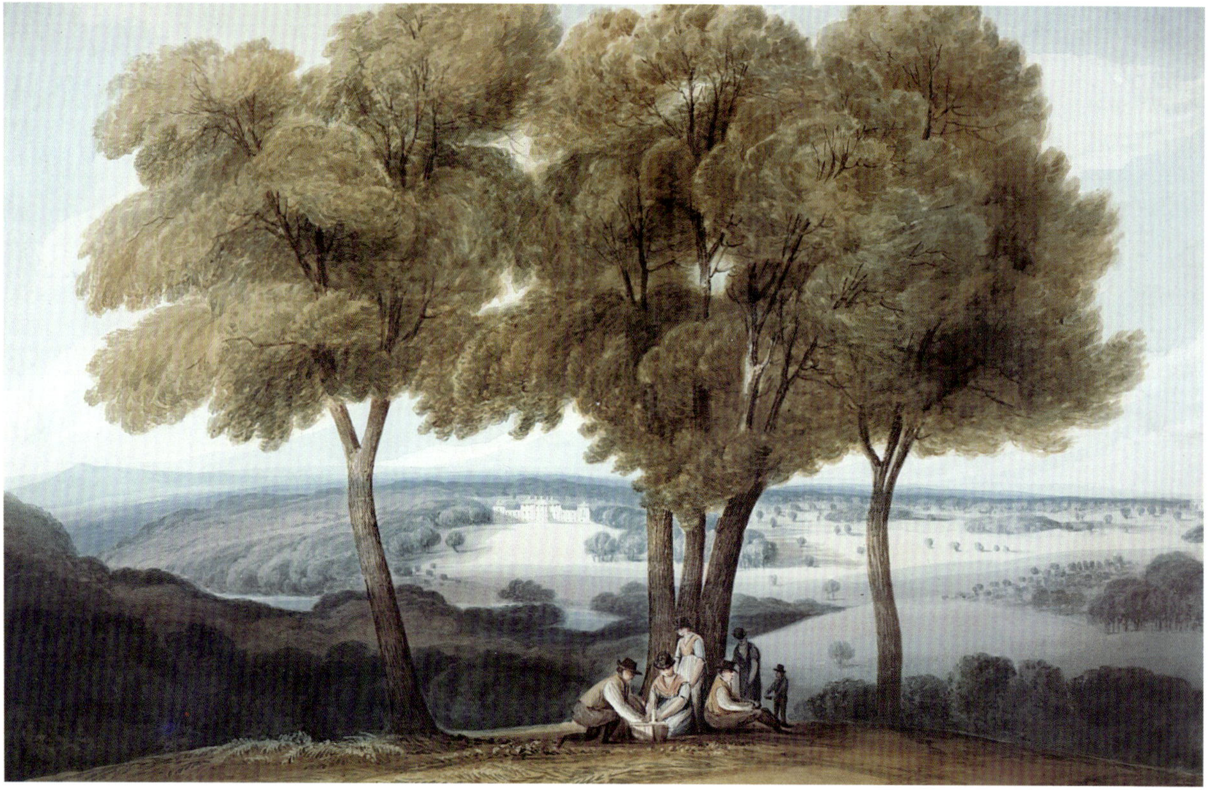

The Presentation of Watercolours at Harewood

by Ann Sumner

Until relatively recently the superb collection of watercolours brought together by Edward Viscount Lascelles including works by Turner, Girtin and Varley were on display in Princess Mary's Sitting-room at Harewood House. However, major refurbishment and re-hanging has meant that they will have two rooms devoted to their display on a rotating basis. Here, light and environmental conditions can be fully controlled and the watercolours better protected for future generations.

Although the watercolours often depict either Harewood House itself or local views, they were not initially hung here by Edward Viscount Lascelles but were instead displayed at Harewood House, Hanover Square, the Lascelles London home. In re-displaying the works here at

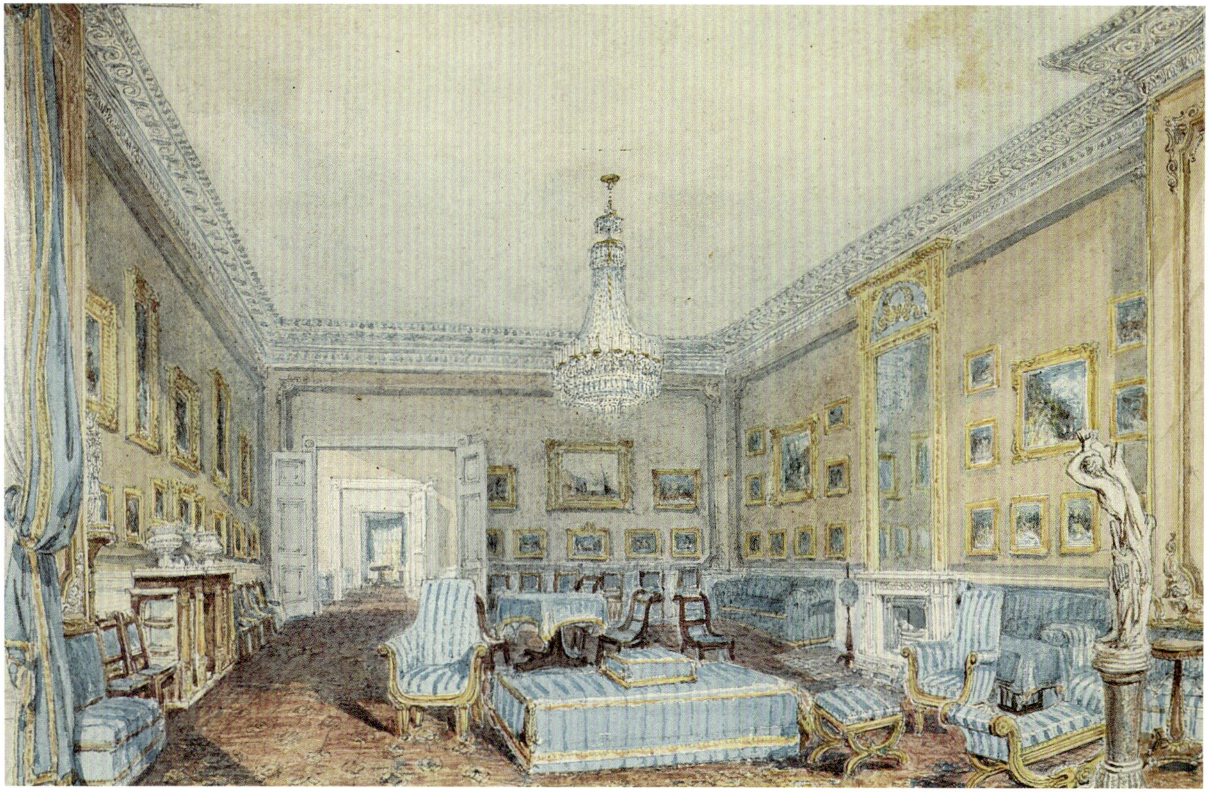

36. J.M.W. Turner – ***Walter Fawkes's exhibition at Grosvenor Place, London,*** *1819. Showing Fawkes's collection of Turner watercolours in period frames. Used as a model for the new display at Harewood. (Mr & Mrs Nicholas Horton-Fawkes)*

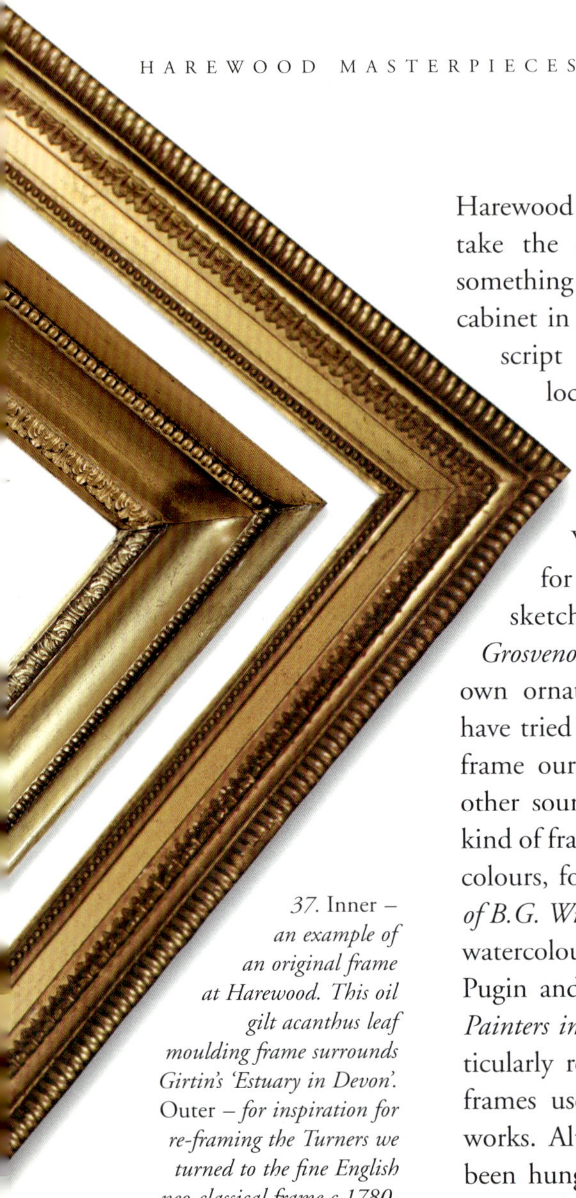

37. Inner – *an example of an original frame at Harewood. This oil gilt acanthus leaf moulding frame surrounds Girtin's 'Estuary in Devon'.* Outer – *for inspiration for re-framing the Turners we turned to the fine English neo-classical frame c.1780-1810. A very rare example enriched with knulling, leaves and pearls.*

Harewood in an historic setting it was decided to take the opportunity to attempt to recreate something of the atmosphere of the connoisseur's cabinet in the early nineteenth century. A manuscript inventory of 1814-20 describes the location of each work, such as in the 'anti-chamber' but we do not unfortunately have a description of the actual hang or a sketch of any of the rooms. We have therefore used as a loose basis for our present hang Turner's very own sketch of *Walter Fawkes's exhibition at Grosvenor Place, London (Ill. 36),* hung with his own ornately framed Turners. In particular we have tried to follow the wall colouring and to re-frame our Turners in period frames. Numerous other sources enable one to gain an idea of the kind of frames which probably enclosed our watercolours, for instance John Scarlett Davis's *Library of B.G. Windus in Tottenham* of 1835, with Turner watercolours framed in a very similar manner and Pugin and Rowlandson's *Gallery of the Society of Painters in Watercolour* of 1808. The latter is particularly relevant because it shows the variety of frames used by watercolourists when exhibiting works. Although our collection is likely to have been hung very much as in the Fawkes London home, they would not all have been in such uniform frames, since a variety of artists painted them and would thus have used different framers.

During the eighteenth century a connoisseur's general practice would have been to collect watercolours and to store them un-framed and in portfolios, thus protecting them from dust and the damaging effect of light but as the century progressed so finished watercolours and drawings were stuck on to stretchers, closely framed and hung in closets throughout the country.[1] Horace Walpole for instance had a display at Strawberry Hill. Writing to Sir Horace Mann in 1753 he stated *'the charming closet where I am now sitting... It is hung with green paper and water-coloured pictures'.*[2] By the time the Society of Painters in Watercolours was formed in 1805 artists such as Turner and Girtin regularly framed their finished watercolours in heavy gilt frames as Pyne described in the *Somerset House Gazette:*

It is only of late that such cabinet productions in this material can be rendered sufficiently rich and deep in tone, to bear out against those broad and superb frames, which seemed alone fitted to the power of oil painting of the same size but experience has proved that watercolours, by the present improved process, have an intensity of depth, and a splendour of effect, which almost raises them to rivalry with cabinet pictures[3].

Some of the watercolours at Harewood are in period frames with scoop mouldings and fairly flat decoration, close-mounted, but these are not necessarily the original frames designed for them. We have documentary evidence of Edward Lascelles paying the frame-maker's bill[4] for *Harewood House from the South East (Ill .17)* and its pair *Harewood House from the South West (Ill. 18).* Since they were in identical period frames, it was assumed that these were the originals. Closer inspection of the frames revealed that the frame of the former seemed to have been made to match that of the latter, which was in any case a very poor fit. The second watercolour remains on its original stretcher and it seems inconceivable that if a frame was made for it, it would not be a good and exact fit. Since both works left the collection in the 1858 sale it is possible that one was re-framed and the other had a frame made to match when it returned. However, the mouldings on the frames are clearly similar to those displayed on some watercolours in the 1808 drawing of the Gallery of the Society of Painters, and thus it was decided to restore these frames and conserve and re-mount the watercolours so that they fitted the frames better.

A similar decision was made with the Varleys, *Harewood House from the North West (Ill. 29)* and *Harewood House from the South West (Ill. 30)* which are displayed in fine late eighteenth century frames with superior carving and moulding to those on the Girtins but which did not fit the watercolours well at all. After under-going conservation the Varleys were mounted in a typical early nineteenth century manner and presented in these frames.

After much debate and consideration it was concluded that only two works at Harewood probably bore their original simple neo-classical frames and they are the small watercolours of an *Estuary in Devon* by Girtin *(Ill. 22)* and *Harewood House from the South East* by Edwin Lascelles *(Ill. 1).* The former is oil gilt over original water gilding with acanthus leaf moulding beneath an internal concave surmounted by a beading and there is a concave moulding to the outside edge. The latter surrounding the Edwin Lascelles is a water gilt frame on pink ground with two lines of acanthus leaf separated by a flat with a concave outer edge. The mounting and framing of these works seems virtually undisturbed.

The most famous watercolours at Harewood are those by Turner and none of these were in period frames. Indeed all appear to have been re-framed in the 1930s and to have acquired large cream mounts. They were indeed the least sympathetically framed of all our watercolours. Turner in particular developed the technical and aesthetic weight of his work to the extent that it could rival the form and gravity of oil painting. For his works, therefore, we tried to find an appropriate moulding close to the two original frames described above. For inspiration we turned to the London Frame-maker Paul Mitchell[5]. From his inventory he proposed a rare English neo-classical frame epitomising the Adam style, and whose ornament is reflected in the Harewood interiors. It has a knulled outer edge, pearl sight edge and applied leaf-and-dart moulding, and is dateable to c.1780-1810 *(Ill. 37)*. This was originally a style applied to watercolours and is identical in size to Turner's larger views of Harewood. This frame bears much more resemblance to our two original frames, described above, than to the more ornate frames in the Fawkes watercolour. Bearing in mind the neo-classical styles of the Girtin and Varley frames, it was decided that it would be more appropriate for the Harewood setting to adopt the pattern suggested by Mr Mitchell, and to commission contemporary hand-carved and water gilded replicas for the Turners. A period, narrower version of this with similar ornament was proposed as a model for the two smaller upright Turners; for the Stevens a further antique frame of the same cross-section with knulling only was reproduced. Girtin's masterpiece *Harewood Bridge (Ill. 24)* was also inappropriately framed, and for this work we chose a late eighteenth century scotia pattern frame carved with ribbon-and-stave and pearls. The weight and design appeared very well suited to the composition and complemented the Turner frames. Thus, by reference to four antique neo-classical frames, we have created an authentic and harmonious presentation of the watercolours in the spirit of the Adam interiors.

The method of display used throughout the nineteenth century of framing finished watercolours and putting them on the walls in direct light soon took its toll on the works themselves and it was rumoured that the watercolours in the Lascelles collection were sold in 1858 because they were fading. Today, in order to re-create an early nineteenth century closet which is conservationally sound, we have put thick blinds at the windows and installed low lighting but we hope still to create the atmosphere of the original setting for such works. Fortunately Princess Mary's Sitting-room here at Harewood was always a fairly dark interior and so the watercolours in the collection are well preserved, especially the colours in the Turners. Labelling throughout has been kept to a minimum to preserve the atmosphere of a connoisseur's cabinet.

Edward Lascelles Collection, Inventory c.1814

Catalogue of Pictures at Harewood House, Hanover Square, London c. 1814 (Leeds City Archives Department, Harewood Papers 520).

This catalogue is an inventory taken on the death of Edward Lascelles, junior, in 1814. The paper is watermarked '*C. Brenchley 1814*' and the catalogue includes portraits by Hoppner of 'the late Lord Lascelles' (No. 35), i.e. Edward, junior, and 'the present Lord Lascelles' (No. 30), i.e. Henry Lascelles, younger brother of Edward, who succeeded as the 2nd Earl of Harewood on his father's death in 1820.

N.B. Annotations on the original manuscript are transcribed here and marked as follows: Those marked in square brackets date from after 1923 and may be associated with Borenius. Those marked in round brackets are valuations connected with the 4th Earl's sale in 1858 where the pictures sold realised similar prices to those marked. The notes following Nos. 47 and 51 are very faint and may be contemporary notes of the loan of those pictures to Lawrence.

Red Room

1. A View in Rome.
2. A View in Rome.
3. A View in Harewood.
4. A Wood Scene. Paul Sandby.
5. A Landscape.
6. (+) A Portrait of Lady Frances Douglas. Cotes
7. A View of Harewood House, [by Varley-passage at Harewood]
8. A Wood Scene, Paul Sandby.
9. A Landscape.
10. A View of Harewood. John Varley.
11. A View of Knaresborough Castle. Girtin(40)
12. A Landscape. Zuccarelli
13. Harewood Castle. De Court.
14. A View of Harewood House. John Varley [passage at Harewood]
15. A view of Plumpton. Girtin. (40) [sold at Christie's in 1920 or 1921 for about £21]

Small Drawing Room

16. (+) A Portrait of Mrs Hale. Cotes [Housekeeper Room, Harewood]
17. A Landscape. Girtin. (20)
18. Guisborough Priory. Girtin .(40)
19. A Landscape. Girtin. (20)
20. Part of the Interior of Westminster Abbey. J.M.W. Turner. (60)
21. (X) A Portrait of Lady Harewood. Cotes. [Sitting Room Harewood]
22. A Ruin. Girtin (30)
23. A Castle, Evening, Havel. (Kilgarren on the Twvy Cardigan Sh. 30)
24. A View on the Wharf. Girtin (20)
25. A Castle, Evening. J.M.W. Turner. (120) * altered from 100
26. An Indian Temple, John Smith. (10)
27. A ruin. Cotman. (20)
28. A Waterfall. John Smith (10)
29. A Waterfall. Callcott. (40)

Large Drawing Room

30. (X) A Portrait of the present Lord Lascelles. Hoppner
31. A View of Harewood Castle J.M.W. Turner (50) [Bt. from Messrs Agnew by Lord Lascelles 1923.]
32. A Corn Field. de Wint. (60)
33. (X) Harewood Castle. J.M.W. Turner. (60) [Given to Lady Hillingdon 1858 left by her to the Hon. Lady Lawrence.]
34. Pembroke Castle. J.M.W. Turner (350)
35. (X) Portrait of the late Lord Lascelles. Hoppner. [Sitting-Room Harewood]
36. A Landscape. John Smith. (20)
37. Part of Windsor Castle. Havel. (30)
38. A Landscape. Callcott. (20)
39. A Mountainous Scene. Girtin. (Beddgelert N. Wales 40)
40. A Ruin. Havel. (20)
41. A View in Switzerland. J.M.W. Turner. (300)
42. A View of Kirkstall Abbey. J.M.W. Turner. (80) [Fitzwilliam Museum, Cambridge.]
43. A View of Windsor and Eton. Callcott. (50)

Anti-Room

44. A Distant View of Harewood Castle. John Varley. (20)
45. A View of Harewood. Girtin. (60) [bought by Lord Penrhyn Given to Lady Louisa Egerton Bought by Lord Lascelles 1919.]
46. (X) A View of Harewood. J.M.W. Turner. (50)
47. (X) A Distant View of Harewood. J.M.W. Turner. (70) (17 June 1822 Sent to Sir Thos Lawrences) [Given to Lady Wharncliffe Given to Lord Lascelles February 28th 1922]
48. A Landscape. Callcott.
49. A Portrait. Holbein [Upper ?Belpan ? Hunt]
50. A View of Snowdon. Callcott
51. A View of Harewood. Girtin (60) (17 June 1822. sent to Sir Thos. Lawrences)
52. (X) A View of Harewood. J.M.W. Turner. (60)
53. (X) A View of Harewood. J.M.W. Turner. (50)
54. A View of Harewood. John Varley. (20)

Breakfast Room

55. A Landscape. Payne.
56. Lady Macbeth. The Baroness De Rous.

57. Family Portraits, a Print, after Hoppner.
58. Family Portraits, a Print, after Hoppner.
59. A Landscape. Payne.
60. A Temple
61. A Sea View. Pocock.
62. A Landscape and Cattle. Pillemens.
63. after Wilson.
64. A View of Snowdon. John Varley.
65. The Precession of the Installation of the Knights of ye Garter. A Print.
66. Italian Figures. Pillemens.
67. A Landscape. Girtin (50)
68. Boats. Girtin. (20)
69. A Group of Cattle. W. Romyn
70. A Landscape. Payne
71. A Village Church and Lane. de Wint. (20)
72. Swiss Peasants. Pillemens.
73. A Waterfall. Girtin. (25)
74. (+) A Pencil Sketch. Girtin (5)
75. A Landscape. Girtin.
76. A Landscape.
77. Harewood Bridge. Girtin. (30)
78. A View near Hampstead. Callcott (20)
79. (+) A Pencil Sketch. Girtin. (5)
80. A Landscape. Payne.
81. A Portrait of Mr. Pitt. after Edridge.
82. (+) A Pencil Drawing. Girtin.(5)
83. A Landscape. Girtin.

Library

84. A Print after Vernet.
85. A Sea Fight after R. Cleverley.
86. A Pencil Drawing. Pillemens
87. A Print after Vernet.
88. A Print after R. Cleverley
89. A Pencil Drawing. Pillemens.

In Lord Harewood's Dressing Room, 2nd, Floor

1. A Tiger, burnt in wood

2-7, 10-12, 17, 21, 23, 28-30, 38, 46, 49, 54-56, 58, 67, 70-72 A Print.

8. A Print of Mrs Kemble.
9. A Print of Mrs Siddons.

13-15, 18-20, 22, 27, 29, 33, 37, 42-45, 48, 50-52, 64 A Drawing.

16. A Print after Barrett.
24. A Drawing by Miss Jane Fleming.
25. A Drawing from Parnell's Hermit by the Baroness De Rous.
26. A Drawing by Cotman.
31. A Print of Mrs Fitzherbert.
32. A Print of Lady Harrington.

35, 36, 40, 41 A Drawing by Payne.

39, 47, 60, 165 A Print after Sir Joshua Reynolds.

Lord Harewood's Dressing Room, Ground Floor

53. (+) A Picture, Vernet.

57, 59, 61-63 A Print, French

66. A Picture.
68. Harewood House
69. A Print, after Peters.

Notes and References

This essay incorporates material from my earlier article, 'A Taste for the Arts: Turner and the patronage of Edward Lascelles of Harewood House' (I & II) which appeared in *Turner Studies* Vol.4, No.2, Winter 1984, and Vol.5, No.1, Spring 1985. The present article expands the discussion of Turner's watercolours at Harewood today, and extends the discussion to Girtin and Varley. The earlier article contains detailed discussion of Turners from the Lascelles collection which have subsequently found homes elsewhere.

1. For a full account of the history and building of the house see Mary Mauchline, *Harewood House,* 1974. For the paintings see T Borenius, *Catalogue of the Pictures and Drawings at Harewood House,* 1936.

2. *The Gentleman's Magazine,* 1795, p.172.

3. K Garlick and A Macintyre (eds), *The Diary of Joseph Farington,* 1978 *et seq.*

4. Farington, *Diary,* 29 August 1801: 'The only pictures are - 4 large pictures by Zucchi, compositions to show Italian manners. Landscapes, views of Knaresborough, Plimpton Rocks, Harwood Castle [etc]. By Sir Joshua Reynolds - Portraits, whole length, late Lord Harwood Do-Do- Lady Harrington, Do-Do- Lady Worsley & Half Length. By Singleton, 1795, Whole Length of Late Lord Harwood. Do of Dowager Lady Harwood. By Hoppner Mrs Yorke daugr. to Lord Harwood, Mrs H Lascelles'.

5. R Warner, *A Tour through the Northern Counties of England and the Borders of Scotland,* 1802, Vol 1, pp.241-2.

6. Borenius *op. cit.* No.360 attributed the watercolour, which is signed 'E LASCELLES 1783', to Edward Lascelles, son of the first Earl of Harewood, presumably on the grounds that he seemed a good candidate, being known to have 'practiced a little'. Borenius misread the date, however as 1793, and ignored an old label (apparently eighteenth century), which reads 'Lady Fleming'. This connects the watercolour to Edwin Lascelles, since Lady Fleming was his wife, they having married in 1770. She survived him to 1813, and the watercolour was presumably marked as her property after Edwin's death in 1795 to avoid confusion with the rest of the Harewood collection which went to Edward Lascelles, later 1st Earl. According to another inscription on the backboard which must have been made after the accession of the first Earl in 1812 (presumably on Lady Fleming's death in 1813), the picture passed to her daughter by a previous marriage, 'The Countess of Harrington/ Harewood House Yorkshire the Seat of the/ Earl of Harewood'. The subsequent history of the watercolour is at present obscure until it was given, as recorded in a label attached to the picture: 'With respectful best wishes/ Mr & Mrs Algernon Hay/ 190/ 17 Chester Sq SW', to the 6th Earl and Princess Mary on their marriage in 1922.

7. Exh RA 1773 No.254. In 1774 Rooker exhibited at the RA No.239 'A view of Harewood Castle, in the county of York, belonging to Edwin Lascelles', which is possibly identifiable with the painting of this subject which currently hangs in the Library at Harewood (Borenius *op. cit.* No.422).

8. Cf. Christie's, London, 9 November 1993, No.17, T Sandby, 'A Journal of a Tour in Yorkshire and Derbyshire [&c]', with illustrations including Harewood House North Front (repr. in catalogue, colour p.24 top left), Harewood House, South Front (repr. colour p.24 lower right).

9. These were bought by the 6th Earl some time before 1936 (see Borenius *op. cit.* Nos 377, 378). It is not known whether they were actually commissioned by Edwin, or whether they previously belonged to the Harewood collection.

10. This observation was first made by Borenius *op. cit.* No.377. Lady Worsley was the daughter of Jane, Lady Fleming, who married Edwin Lascelles in 1770, after which she might have been a visitor to Harewood at almost any time. Lady Worsley married Sir Richard Worsley in 1775 and was a celebrated beauty and socialite, and sat to Sir Joshua Reynolds in June 1779. Since Malton was at Harewood the previous year, 1778, it is perfectly possible that he could have seen her wearing the same distinctive red outfit. In 1781 she was the *cause célèbre* of a scandalous infidelity, and the portrait, presumably commissioned by her husband, was dispatched to her stepfather, Edwin Lascelles, instead.

11. For Turner in general see A. J. Finberg, *Life of J.M.W. Turner,* 2nd ed 1961. For Turner's association with Malton, loc. cit., pp. 17-18. There seems to be relatively little known with any certainty about the connection between Turner and Malton, but see note 40 below.

12. Leeds City Archives Department, Harewood papers, Calendar numbers: 189-192, Edward Lascelles *the younger,* 1795 - 1814; 212 Edward, *the elder,* 1790 - 1797; 211 Edward, the elder, 1796 - 1800.

13. (212), 21 January 1790

14. The artist christened his son Lascelles Hoppner and Edward Lascelles was one of the sponsors. Shortly after inheriting the Harewood fortune in 1795 Lascelles commissioned a clutch of portraits from Hoppner and even shared with the painter some of his good fortune, making a gift of £15.7.6 on 19 October 1795, (212).

15. (212), 2 July 1790

16. (212), 1 May 1795. The Harewood collection contains one example of the work of John Glover, a watercolour of a *Welsh Mountain Lake,* signed and dated 1803. According to Borenius *op. cit.* No.314, this was bought before 1936 by the 6th Earl 'From the collection of the Duchess of Grafton'.

17. (212), 1 June 1795

18. (211), 14 June 1798. The Plompton oils are discussed fully in my 1984 *Turner Studies* article *op. cit.* part II, pp.30-33.

19. Farington, *op. cit.* 25 January 1795

20. Farington, *op. cit.* 14 November 1795

21. (189), 6,13 September and 12 October 1795

22. (189). There are a number of payments to Daniell in the account books, including £31.0.0 for 'two Drawings Views in India' on 21 November 1797 (189). The remainder are for prints and various parts of his subscription series of 'Oriental Views'. There are no watercolours identified as his in the 1814 Inventory or 1858 sale catalogue.

23. (189). Paul Sandby (1725 - 1809) has been referred to as 'the father of English watercolour' for his pioneering role in using colour more solidly than had generally been the case, and on a larger scale. The 1814 Inventory lists two *Wood Scenes* (nos. 4, 8) and the 1858 sale included (lot 25) 'A Landscape, with a River' and (lot 27) 'A Wood scene, with figures felling timber'. Several watercolours of Windsor by Paul Sandby are noted in Borenius *op. cit.* nos. 427 - 32. Nos 427-30 were presented to Princess Mary as a wedding present in 1922 by Sir Richard Molynaux KCVO.

24. (189). The Inventory lists three items by William Payne (fl.1776 - 1803), all 'Landscapes', together with 4 'Drawings' in Lord Harewood's 2nd floor dressing room, nos.35,36,40,41. The 1858 sale included (lot 7) 'A Seaport and a landscape, a pair', and (lot 12) 'A view of Harewood House'.

25. (189)

26. (191), 20 August 1799

27. See e.g. A Wilton, 'The Monro School Question: Some Answers', *Turner Studies,* Vol.4, no.2, Winter 1984, pp. 8-23. There are two examples of Monro school work by Turner in the Harewood collection, cf. Borenius *op. cit.* nos. 473, 474.

28. T Girtin and D Loshak, *The Art of Thomas Girtin,* 1954, p.22.

29. (189)

30. The whereabouts of this watercolour seems to have been unknown to modern Turner scholarship, and it is here reproduced for the first time. It is listed as untraced by Andrew Wilton, *Life and Work of J.M.W.Turner,* 1979 as no. 122. It was engraved by J Greig and published in 1804 in his *Views of London and its Environs.* It was listed by Sir W Armstrong, Turner, 1902, where he noted its appearance in 'W Ward's catalogue, No.III, supplement'. W.G.Rawlinson, *The Engraved Work of J.M.W.Turner,* 2 Vols, 1907, i.p.30 No.72 remarks: 'The drawing, much faded, was sold a few years ago by Mr W Ward'. It will be realised that there are a number of significant differences of detail between the watercolour and the engraving, which would suggest that Greig exercised his artistic license to achieve, it might be admitted, a superior sense of space and atmosphere in the engraving. The watercolour is somewhat faded and damaged and might well have been originally more convincing in these areas. Turner's detail of the castle, however, seems to be rather more accurate than its transcription in the engraving. A similar composition by Thomas Girtin is reproduced in R Davis *Thomas Girtin's Watercolours,* 1924, Pl.67. Girtin and Loshak *op. cit.* No.279 record it in the Hickman Bacon collection, and speculate that it was inspired by a composition by John Robert Cozens.

31. Cf. my discussion of Turner's first exhibit at the Royal Academy, *The Archbishop's Palace, Lambeth* [sic], 1790, in *Turner on the Thames,* 1993, and also in 'When Panting Art Toils after Truth in Vain', the 15th Kurt Pantzer Memorial Lecture, Turner Society News, no.67, August 1994, p.11 ff.

32. Wilton *op. cit.* 1979 No.138, and *Turner Studies,* 4.ii, p.26

33. *Turner Studies* 4.ii p.27 and Wilton 1979 Nos.182 ff.

34. Turner Bequest, Tate Gallery, London, TB XXXIV, XXXV

35. Turner Bequest, Tate Gallery, London, TB XXXIV 67 - 76, TB LI L,R,S,T,U,V,W,X,Y, TB CXCVII L

36. *Turner in Yorkshire,* catalogue of the exhibition at York City Art Gallery, 1980, No.11.

37. Turner Bequest, Tate Gallery, TB LI R

38. *The Times,* 3 May 1797

39. (189), 21 November 1797

40. Given that we do not know much with any certainty about Turner's relationship with Malton (see n.11, above), this particular piece of evidence seems not to have been given as much weight as it perhaps deserves. It suggests that the association was rather longer lasting than the brief attendance at a school, c.1789-90, run by Malton as most chroniclers have supposed. At the very least it indicates a significant Master/ pupil relationship and a definite perception of their relative status at this time.

41. Girtin and Loshak, *op. cit.* p.101. The reference is not to Malton specifically, but Girtin and Loshak develop a particularly interesting argument regarding Girtin's tendency to abstraction being indicative of larger socio-cultural forces at work. This will repay careful consideration, and has been influential in the present account.

42. Cf. e.g. Finberg *op. cit.* 1961 p. 98 ff on Turner's exhibits of 1803.

43. (189), 15 March 1798

44. The watercolour was given by the 4th Earl to his sister Louisa Lascelles, and has descended in the family to the present owner.

45. Turner Bequest, Tate Gallery, London, TB XXXIV inside cover, cf. *Turner Studies,* 4.ii p.29. The name of 'Wm Blake' is inscribed on the back of the sketch. This is probably William Blake of Portland Place who is known as a patron of Turner at this time (see *Turner Studies,* 4.ii, p.32, n.31, and 5.i, p.46, n.19). The Harewood watercolour was exhibited at Agnews in 1955 No.22 as 'Hornby Castle', and sold by them to H.R.H.Princess Royal in 1957.

46. An oil painting closely related to the small watercolour at Harewood was sold at Phillips, London in 1988 as 'circle of J.M.W.Turner' and exhibited at the Northern Antiques Fair at Harrogate by Leger Galleries in 1993. Although the oil has been accepted by some Turner scholars, it does not seem likely to the present author that Turner himself would have repeated the composition so closely.

47. J Jewell, *The Tourist's Companion or the History and Antiquities of Harewood in Yorkshire,* 1818, p.54

48. Cf *Turner Studies* 5.i, p.33 ff

49. (192), 8 April 1806

50. (192)

51. Turner Bequest, Tate Gallery, TB CII 21

52. Now in a private collection, on loan to the Art Gallery of Toronto, Canada. See D.Hill, *Turner in the Alps,* 1992, p.76.

53. Turner Bequest, Tate Gallery, London, *Derbyshire* sketchbook, TB CVI 87a-83a.

54. The standard work on Girtin is Girtin and Loshak, *op. cit.* 1954. The two most recent works are F. Hawcroft, *Watercolours by Thomas Girtin,* catalogue of the exhibition at the Whitworth Art Gallery, Manchester and Victoria and Albert Museum, London, 1975, and Susan Morris, *Thomas Girtin, 1775-1802,* catalogue of the exhibition at the Yale Centre for British Art, New Haven, USA, 1986.

55. First cited in W. Thornbury, *Life of J.M.W.Turner,* 1862, i.117

56. (191), 21 November 1798

57. J. L. Roget, *History of the Old Watercolour Society,* 1891, i,96

58. Farington, *op. cit.* 9 February 1799

59. Borenius 1936 p.vi, n.1 mentions a memorandum 'of the several improvements hinted or stated by Mr Repton during his visit at Harewood, August 1800', which included: 'Views from the House - The General sweeping lines of woods are described in a sketch made by Mr Girtin and altered from the Portico'. The drawing has not been identified.

60. (189), 17 February 1798

61. (191), 9 May 1798

62. (191), 21 November 1798

63. (191), 15 February 1799

64. (191), 15 January 1800

65. (191) 17 February 1801

66. Roget *op cit,* i 110, 120 (where date given as July)

67. *Harewood House from the South East* was included in the 1858 sale (No.39) where bought by 'Col. Pennant' for 20 gns. It was subsequently given by Lord Penrhyn to Lady Louisa Egerton (Cavendish), and acquired by the 6th Earl of Harewood in 1919. *Harewood House from the South West* was No.22 in the 1858 sale where it was bought by 'Palser' for 15 gns. It was subsequently owned by E Cohen and E Poulter before being bought by the 6th Earl, sometime before 1936. Borenius *op. cit.*, No.307 does not give the date of acquisition. The two other watercolours of the group of four paid for in 1801 are identifiable as *Knaresborough* (signed and dated 1801) in the Whitworth Art Gallery, Manchester (Girtin and Loshak *op. cit.*, No.436), and *Plompton Rocks* in the Victoria and Albert Museum, London (p.129-1920, Girtin and Loshak *op. cit.* No.271). Each is of the same scale as the Harewood pair, and show unusual distinguishing characteristics - see note following. At 2 feet by 3, these watercolours, together with *Near Beddgelert* (Private Collection - Girtin and Loshak *op. cit.*, No.266), also from the Lascelles collection, constitute Girtin's largest works, apart from his panoramas.

68. Examination by the author, together with Dr Ann Sumner and paper conservator Jane Milward, at Harewood in October 1994 revealed that Girtin's *Harewood House from the South East* was glued to a stretcher. Traces of colour all around the stretcher suggest that this could be the condition in which Girtin finished it. *Harewood House from the South West* by Girtin had been removed from its stretcher, attached to a backing sheet, and taped back to the stretcher on the reverse side. Again there are clear signs of the stretcher wood being overwashed all round. The edges of both drawings have been nicked and tucked around the edges, presumably to eliminate the effect of cockling when the sheets were glued to the wood. Both *Plompton Rocks* at the Victoria and Albert Museum, and *Knaresborough* at the Whitworth Art Gallery, Manchester, exhibit similar features. In all cases it appears that washes of colour have been laid over the cuts and have soaked into them. *Knaresborough* was restored in 1981 and the conservator's report at the Whitworth records that the painting was found backed onto a thicker brown/black paper and then mounted to a wooden stretcher with tacks and animal glue. The stretcher was removed and disposed of. It is not obvious whether the stretcher is present or not in *Plompton Rocks.*

69. Although the frames for *Harewood House from the South West* and *Harewood House from the South East* were superficially similar, the latter was very much a botched fit and the former seems to have been made to match. The two large Varleys of *Harewood House from the North West* and *Harewood House from the South West* were again in superficially similar frames, but the watercolours again fitted badly. The frames are nevertheless appropriate to the period and have been reused. The history of the framing and presentation of watercolours is discussed by Jane Bayard in *Works of Splendor and Imagination: The Exhibition Watercolor 1770 - 1870,* catalogue of the exhibition at the Yale Centre for British Art, New Haven, USA, 1981. The principles of original presentation were in part implemented in Andrew Wilton's exhibition, *The Great Age of British Watercolours* at the Royal Academy, London, in 1993, and have been further explored by Corinne Miller in the exhibition of *Still Waters: Watercolours from Leeds City Art Galleries* at Leeds City Art Gallery, 1995.

70. There is another version of *Grimbald Bridge* in the Shepherd sketchbook at the Whitworth Art Gallery, Manchester. The two versions are remarkably alike. There is another example of such close similarity between the composition of *Middleham* in the Shepherd sketchbook and the same image in Leeds City Art Gallery (13. 113/53). In both cases it would appear that (inscriptions excepted) one is an improbably faithful replica of the other, attempting to reproduce every nuance of pressure and autographic idiosyncrasy. In both cases the attempt has been impressively successful, but close examination will reveal numerous slight discrepancies throughout. It is perhaps significant that Thomas Girtin's brother, John Girtin, who settled ultimately in Pudsey, Leeds, was a printmaker and a rogue (see Girtin and Loshak *op. cit.* p.123). A further page of the Shepherd sketchbook shows *Harewood House from the South* and is inscribed 'Harewood House 1800'. A note on the margin of the opposite page reads 'Sketch of Harewood House in pencil sold to Mr Hargreaves £1.1.0' which is possibly identifiable with the drawing at Yale (see n.67 below). Girtin and Loshak *op. cit.*, No.367 note: 'A watercolour bearing the above title was sold in the Percy sale, Christie's, 22.4.1890 (313), bt by Colnaghi, £11'. Another page shows *Hall Stables, Plompton Park* (Girtin and Loshak *op. cit.*, no.374). For the Shepherd sketchbook in general see M Hardie, 'A sketchbook of Thomas Girtin', *Walpole Society,* 27 (1938): pp. 88-95. The pages are not now in the order catalogued by Hardie.

71. There is another pencil sketch of *Harewood House* by Girtin at the Yale Centre for British Art in New Haven, USA (B.1975.3.11.1192.). The Yale Centre contains another Girtin associated with Harewood, a *Temple in Harewood Park,* (B.1975.3.1193).

72. An inscription in the Inventory of c.1814 against No.51 records that this composition was lent to Sir Thomas Lawrence on 17 June 1822 as reference for the background to his portrait of *Henry Lascelles, 2nd Earl of Harewood,* which was exhibited at the R.A. in 1823. The use Lawrence made of the Girtin can be examined in the portrait at Harewood (Borenius *op. cit.*, No. 365).

73. The watercolour was exhibited at Agnews in 1935, no.143 as 'Dover Harbour', and bought from them, according to a label on the back, by the 6th Earl in March 1937. The label also says that 'This picture was formerly at Harewood House, Hanover Square'. According to Girtin and Loshak *op. cit.* No.409 (where it is dated c.1800!) it appeared in the 1858 sale (?Lot 15 A Harbour Scene with Shipping, bt Palser £5.0.0) and was subsequently in the collections of E Cohen and E Poulter. The identification with No.60 'Boats' in the 1814 Inventory seems a little problematic in view of the valuation of '20' which seems rather high for such a modestly-sized watercolour.

74. Girtin and Loshak, *op. cit.*, pp.29-30

75. Sotheby's, London, 21 November 1985 (102) repr. catalogue in black and white. Owen exhibited between 1794 and 1810 at the Royal Academy, and from 1808 at the Associated Artists in Watercolour. It is not known whether he had any contact with Girtin directly, but his membership of the Associated Artists in Watercolour ties him into a network of painters with whom Girtin would have had some contact, and on whom he would have had some influence.

76. Morris *op. cit.*, p.22, postulates a West Country tour for Girtin in 1800 or 1801, and exhibits (nos. 86, 87) two watercolours which bear comparison with the Harewood picture. It is tempting to surmise some common interest in the West Country with Edward Lascelles, given the Devon subjects in the album of the latter's drawings at Harewood.

77. Cf Borenius *op. cit.*, no.309 'Landscape...never left Harewood'.

78. John Ruskin, *Modern Painters,* IV, 1856, p.246

79. Girtin and Loshak, *op. cit.*, passim

80. There were a number of important north of England subjects in the Lascelles collection, including *Lodore Falls* (Ashmolean Museum, Oxford), *On the Wharfe* (Victoria and Albert Museum), *Ilkley* (Leeds City Art Gallery), *Bamburgh Castle* (Tate Gallery, London) and *Knaresborough Castle* (Whitworth, Manchester).

81. Turner Bequest, Tate Gallery, London, TB XXXV 70

82. 1801 would seem to be an appropriate date in stylistic terms. The limited colour range can be compared to the *Ilkley* in Leeds City Art Gallery, which seems also to originate from the Lascelles collection and is inscribed on the reverse 'Mr Lascelles'.

83. Cf. e.g. Adele M Holcomb, *John Sell Cotman at the British Museum,* 1978; Miklos Rajnai, *John Sell Cotman 1782- 1842,* catalogue of the exhibition at the Victoria and Albert Museum, London [&c], 1982-3, and Corinne Miller, *Cotmania and Mr Kitson,* catalogue of the exhibition at Leeds City Art Gallery, 1993.

84. No.27 'A Ruin'. This was valued at '20' in the presale valuations inscribed on the Inventory, and must therefore have been a considerable work. It appeared in the 1858 sale as no.38, 'A ruined abbey - upright', where it was bought by 'Mitchell' for 7 gns. It had not yet proved possible to identify this with any certainty. The Inventory also records no.26 in Lord Harewood's Dressing Room, 'A Drawing'.

85. These are given by Borenius *op. cit.* nos 361, 362, 363, and p.vi to Edward Lascelles the younger, on no other grounds than that they seem 'Girtinesque' and he wants to prove some effect of Girtin's teaching on Lascelles. These drawings are not at all like Girtin, and not at all like the work of Edward Lascelles as it is known in the album at Harewood.

86. The negative spaces are a distinctive feature of Cotman's work in both pencil and watercolour from this period. In pencil, it is quite an unusual approach, suggesting an origin in the stopping-out techniques of watercolour popular at this time, and central to Cotman's work. See, for example, Cotman's drawings of *The Bridgewater Seapiece, after Turner* in the British Museum (1902.5.14.284, Holcomb *op. cit.*, no.5), *Tree Study,* c.1804, (BM 1902.5.14.309, Holcomb no.16), *Larch Trees at Brandsby,* c.1805, (BM 1902.5.14.293, Holcomb no.17), *Head of a Man in Van Dyck Dress,* c.1807 (BM 1902.5.14.15, Holcomb no.31), *On the Greta,* 1805, (Leeds, Miller no.14) and *Brignall Banks,* 1805, (Leeds, Miller no.17).

87. Roget *op. cit.*, i.166

88. Roget *op. cit.*, i.168. For Varley in general see C M Kauffmann, *John Varley 1778 - 1842,* Victoria and Albert Museum and Batsford, 1984, and Anne Lyles, 'John Varley's Early Work', *Journal of the Old Watercolour Society Club,* 59th Annual Volume, 1984, although neither source discusses Varley's Harewood watercolours.

89. (191), 16 March 1801. This is an exceptionally generous sum for a single drawing. Kauffmann *op. cit.*, p.33 observes that in 1805 two 'exceptionally large and imposing Welsh subjects' by Varley fetched 10 gns and 8 gns at the Society of Painters in Watercolour exhibition. The price books for the Society of Painters in Watercolours in the National Art Library at the Victoria and Albert Museum, London (MS L[-] 1868, 86 BB 41-45, 47, 48) reveal that a 'Mr Lascelles' paid Varley 20 gns for a watercolour of 'Flint Castle', No.11 at the exhibition of 1808. This is not recorded in the 1814 Inventory.

90. Roget *op. cit.*, i.172. The British Museum has a number of sketches relating to Varley's Yorkshire tour of 1803.

91. One is Borenius *op. cit.* No.475. The other was bought by the present Earl in the West Indies, where presumably it had been sent some time ago to one of the family properties.

92. Kauffmann *op. cit.* p.24 remarks on Varley's reliance on traditional eighteenth century precedents for his compositions and viewpoints.

93. Farington, *Diary,* 2 November 1802

94. Borenius *op. cit.*, No.331

95. This might lead us to speculate that this pair of Varleys was bought by Henry Lascelles and not Edward. There is some scope in the recorded pictures to allow this. Edward's Inventory records five Varley watercolours of Harewood subjects, but there are in fact six that survive to us. It seems possible that there is another composition yet to be discovered.

96. The backboard bears a modern Agnew's label with the stock number 39810. There is also an early nineteenth century label of 'Ford and Dickenson/ Carvers and Gilders/ 129 Wardour Street'. The frame has been used as a model in reframing the companion watercolour by Varley of *Harewood House from the South East.*

97. Varley's view of *Harewood House from the South East* is most closely related to Turner's sketch of the view, TB LI L, which shows the same farm in the foreground. A version of the same view by Abraham Wood was engraved by S. Brown and published as the frontispiece to J. Jewell's *The Tourist's Companion or the History and Antiques of Harewood, Yorkshire,* Leeds, 1818, (repr. Turner's Studies, 4.i. p.32, pl.19) and a further version of the same view, probably also by Abraham Wood was recently with Agnew (Stock number 4649).

98. See Jean Hamilton, *The Sketching Society 1799 - 1851,* catalogue of the exhibition at the Victoria and Albert Museum, 1971.

99. Including *A Treatise of the Principles of Landscape Design,* 1821

100. Borenius *op. cit.*, Nos. 478, 479, bequeathed to the 6th Earl in 1916 by the Marquess of Clanricarde. Kauffmann *op. cit.*, no.79, 'Landscape sketch of rocks and trees' in the V&A (Dyce 950) is closely related to the Harewood composition of *Landscape with Figures,* in both general terms and also in specific detail. Painted in a much freer manner than the Harewood picture, it might almost be considered as the basis of it. Another watercolour at the V&A (P50-1919 - Kauffmann No.75) is dated 1841 like the Harewood watercolour, and can be closely compared in terms of style and subject-matter.

101. Particularly the de Wints, Callcotts and Havells. de Wint's No.48 'A Cornfield with many figures' fetched £108.3.0, which is more than some of the Turners.

102. Borenius *op. cit.*, p.vii.

Notes and references from *'The Presentation of Watercolours at Harewood'* by Ann Sumner.

1. Further information about the framing of watercolours at this time is given by Jane Bayard. Quoted Yale *op. cit.*, pp.25-33.
2. Horace Walpole, *Selected Letters of Horace Walpole,* ed. US Lewis 1973 p.44.
3. *Somerset House Gazette II* p.46.
4. Letter of 27 June 1801 written by Edward Lascelles to Girtin referring to frame-makers for two of Girtin's frames. Roget *op. cit.* i. 110, 120.
5. I would like to thank Paul Mitchell and Neil Trinder, who have been working on the Harewood frames, for their invaluable help and advice in preparing this paper.

Our thanks are extended to Dr David Hill for his tireless research on the Lascelles family patronage of watercolourists; to Viscountess Lascelles for her suggestions and continuous support; to Dr Ann Sumner for curating the display and so enthusiastically co-ordinating the project with her assistant Sally Wilks; to Neil Trinder for the restoration of frames; to Mr Paul Mitchell for the making of period replica frames; to Jane Milward and Keith Holmes for their conservation work on the watercolours, and to Paul McTague for help in remounting; to Sue Morris, Miklos Rajnai and Amanda Kirkpatrick for their help with research.

Our thanks also to Andrew Esson for his design of this book; to Michael Hockney and his colleagues at Christies, to Andrew Hirst and his colleagues at Watmoughs Financial Print for their careful attention to detail; to Jim Kershaw, Clare Arron and Hugh Palmer for their painstaking photography; to Carlotta Gelmetti, Joanna Wallace and James Kelvington for photographic reproduction; to Ivan Lister, Robert Kay, and Hensons for the re-decoration of the watercolour rooms and to Jane Croudson for the making of curtains.

Other permanent members of staff have been extremely helpful and special thanks go to Judith Wrench, Diane Holloway, Alison Sherlock and Brenda Grant. Finally, and by no means least, our gratitude is specially extended to Christie's for their generous sponsorship of this book and to Watmoughs for printing it. Without this we would not have been able to produce such a fine publication. – **Terence Suthers**, *Director, Harewood House Trust*